THE
OLIVE FAIRY BOOK

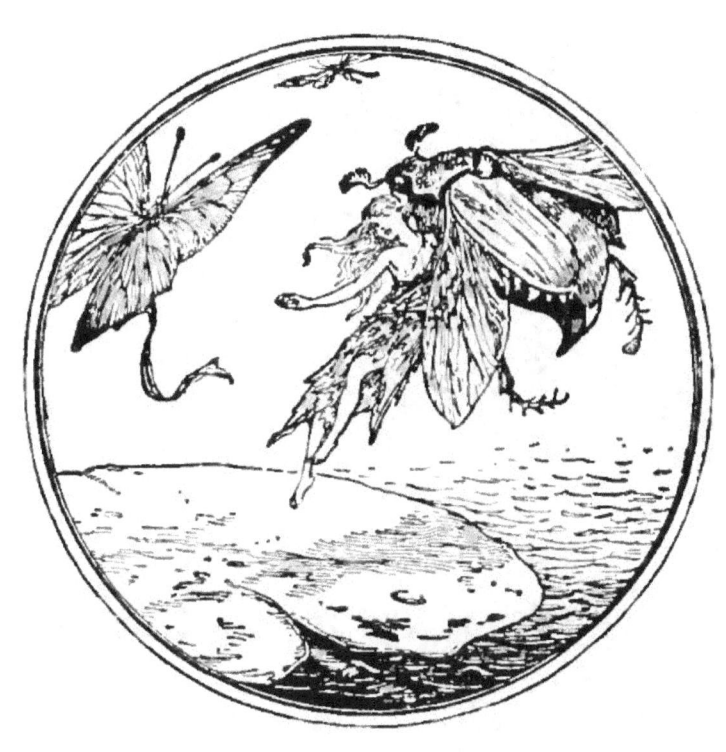

WITH
NUMEROUS ILLUSTRATIONS BY H. J. FORD

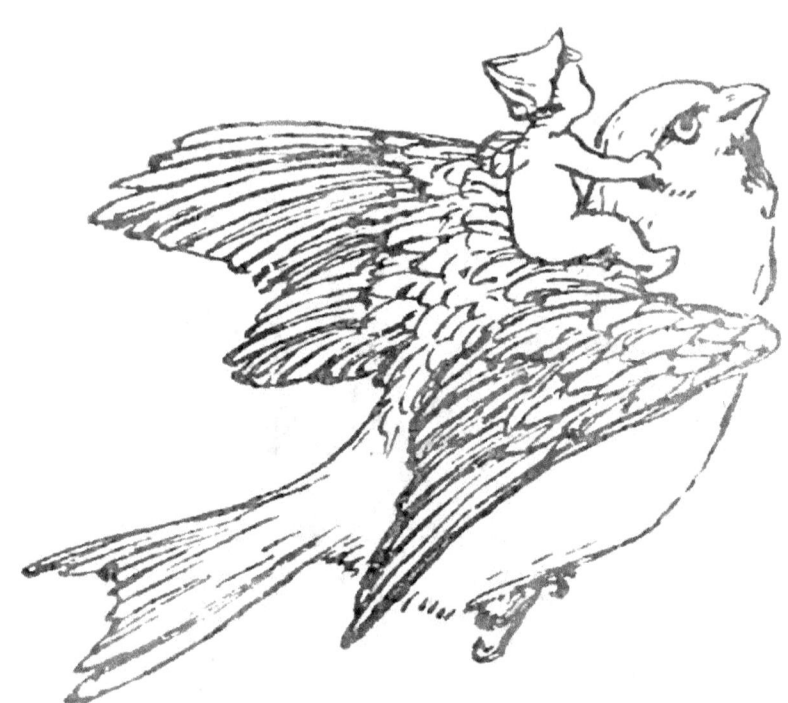

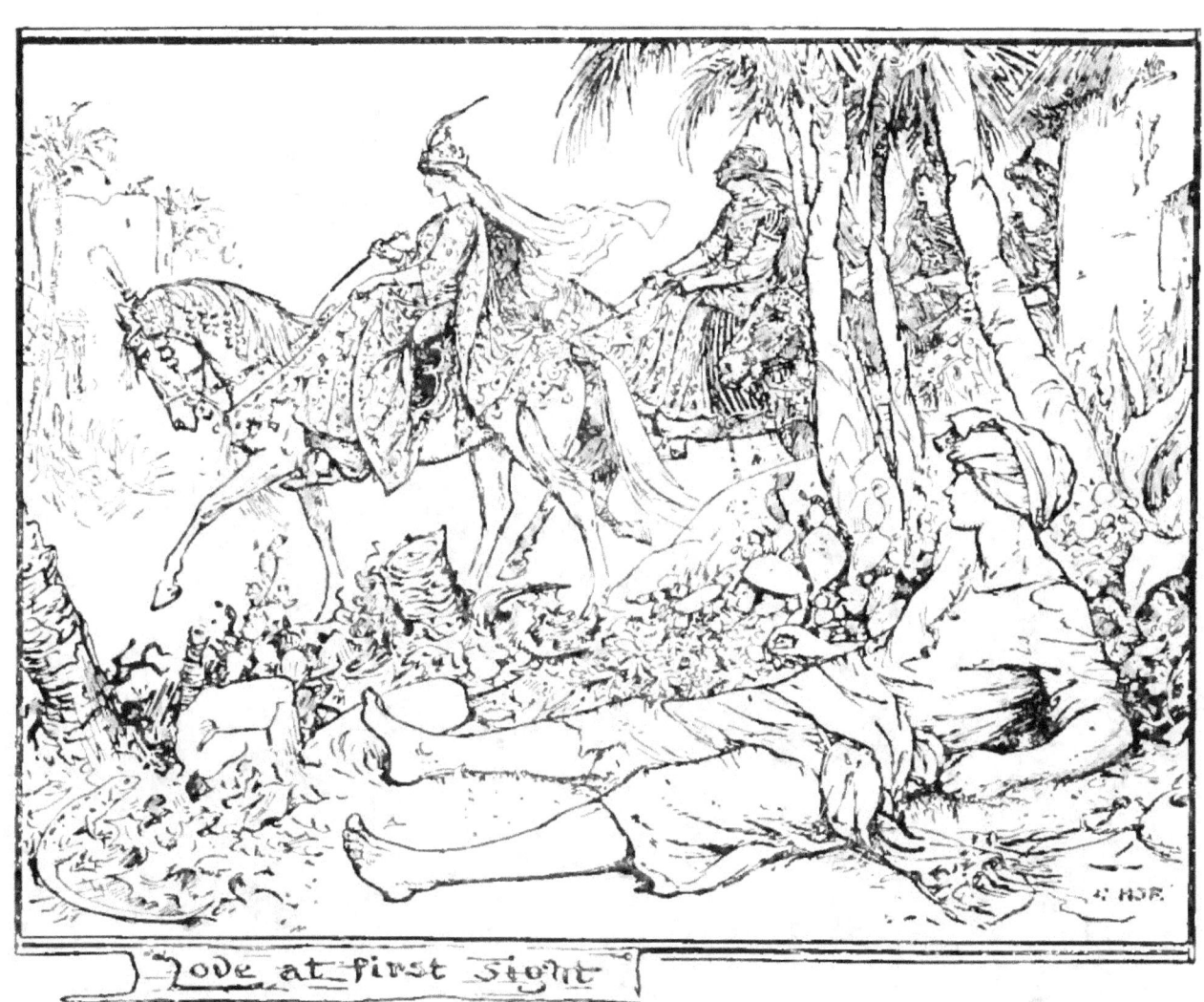
Love at first Sight

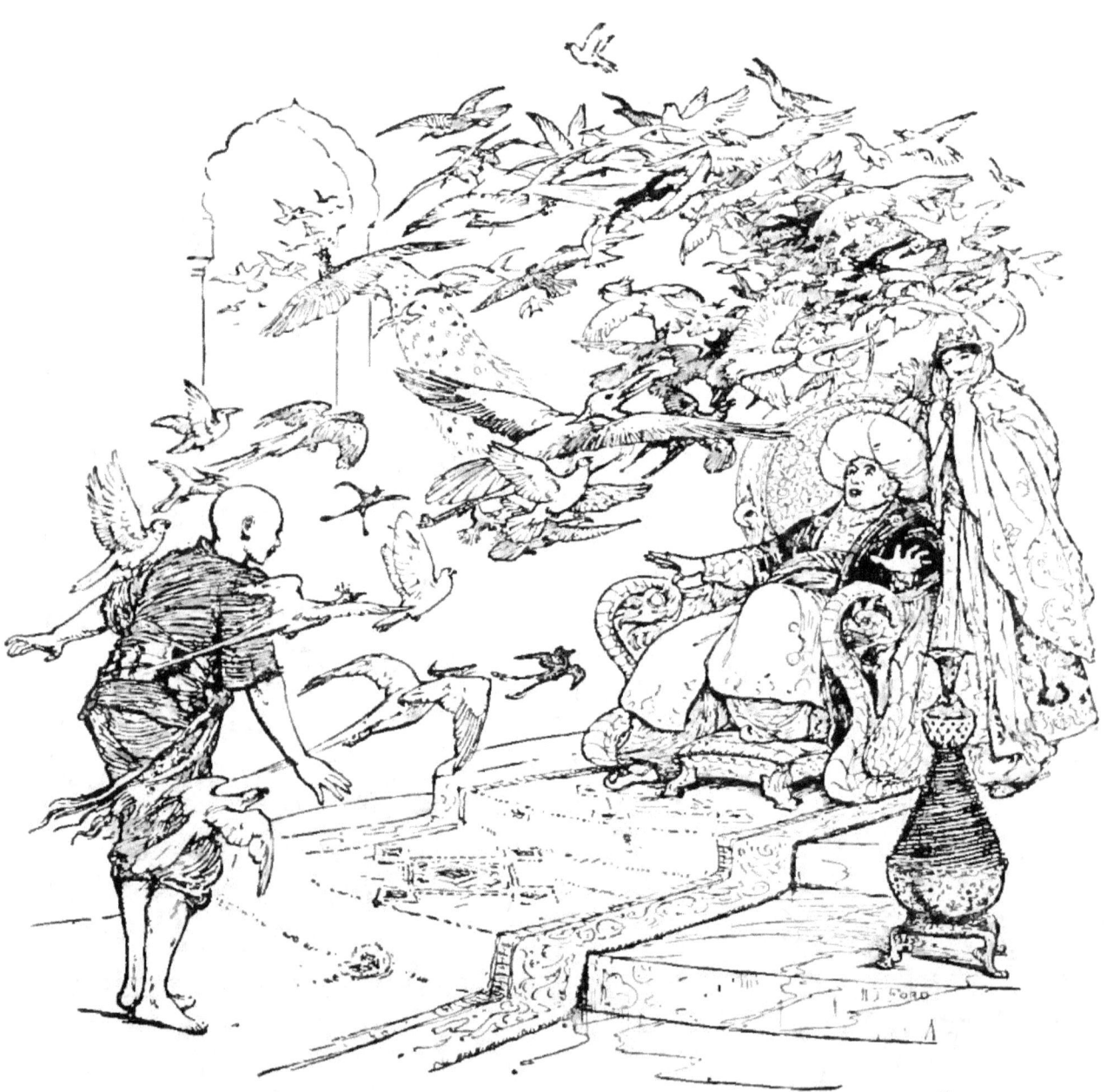

How the BIRDS were brought to the SULTAN

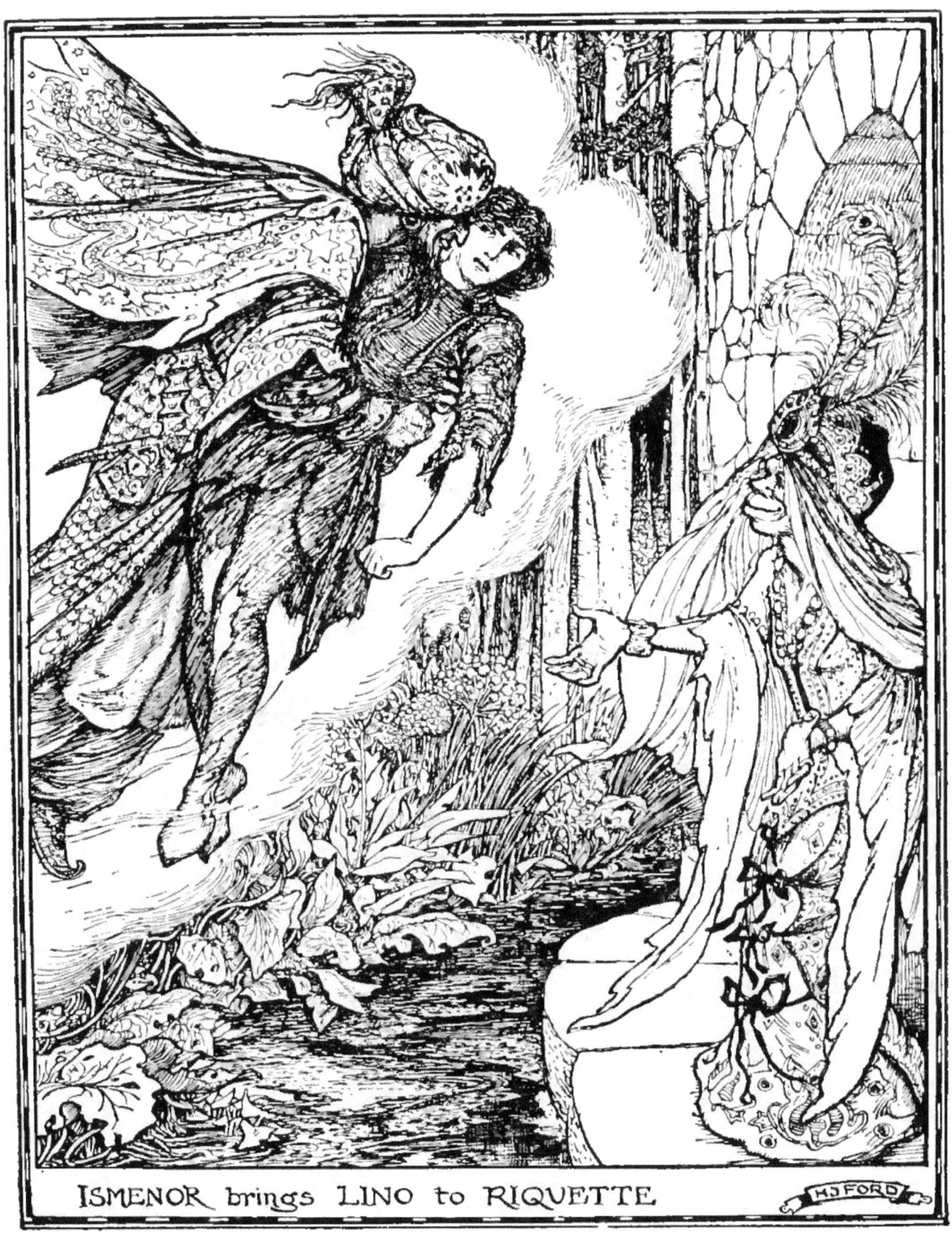
ISMENOR brings LINO to RIQUETTE

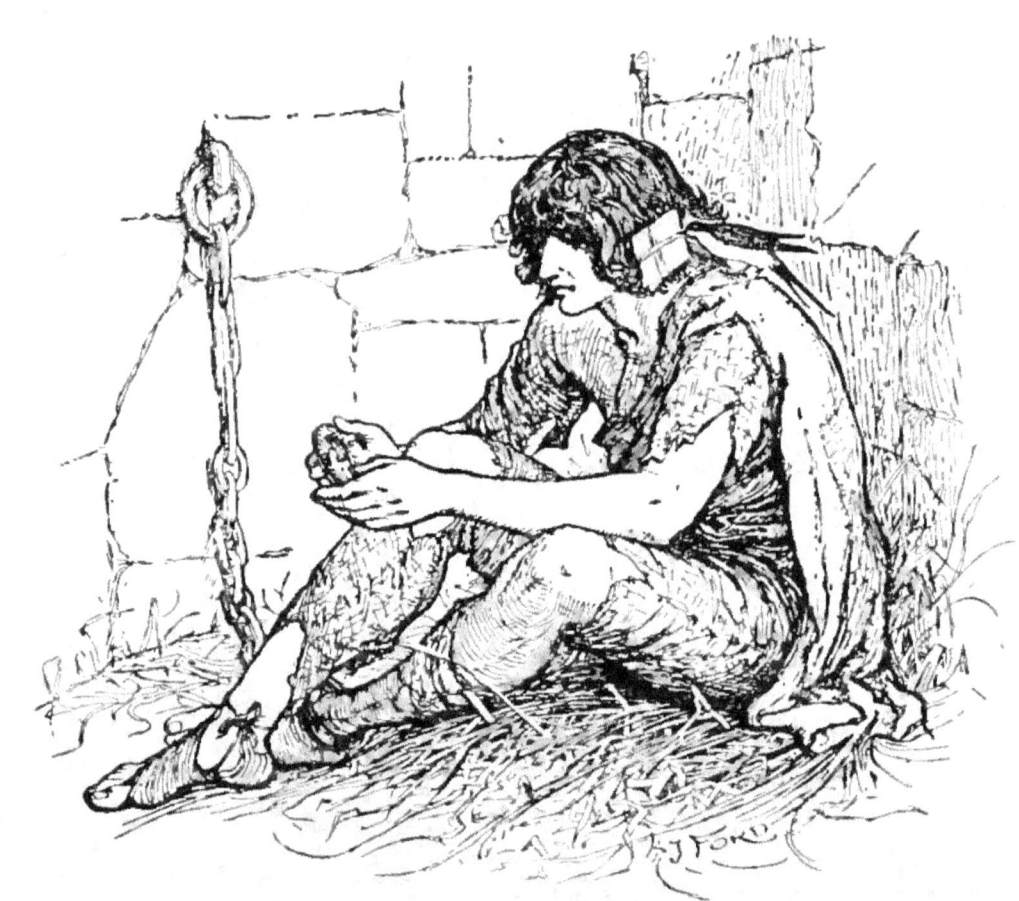
THE SWALLOW BRINGS THE NOTE TO LINO

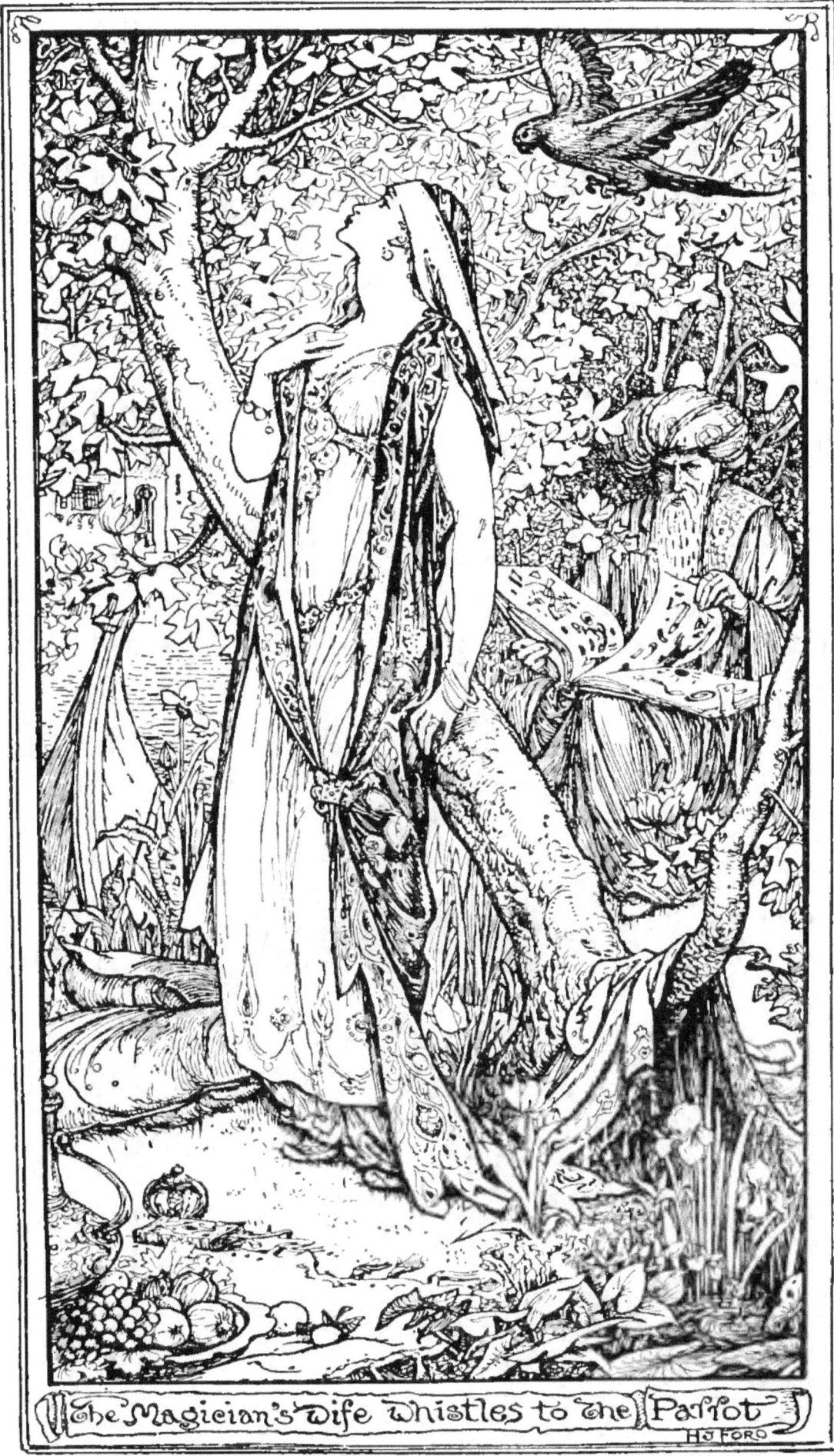
The Magician's Wife Whistles to the Parrot

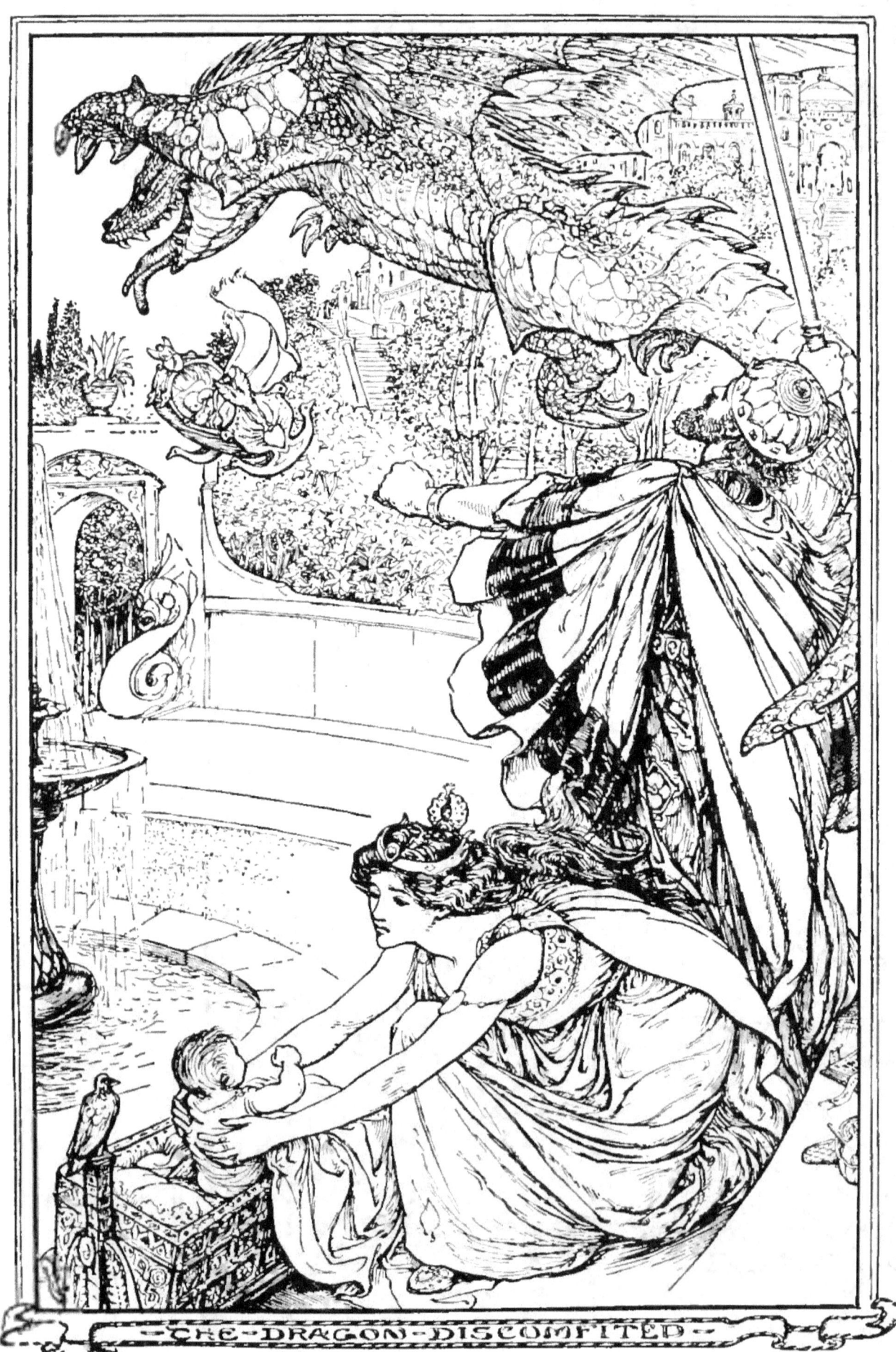
THE DRAGON DISCOMFITED

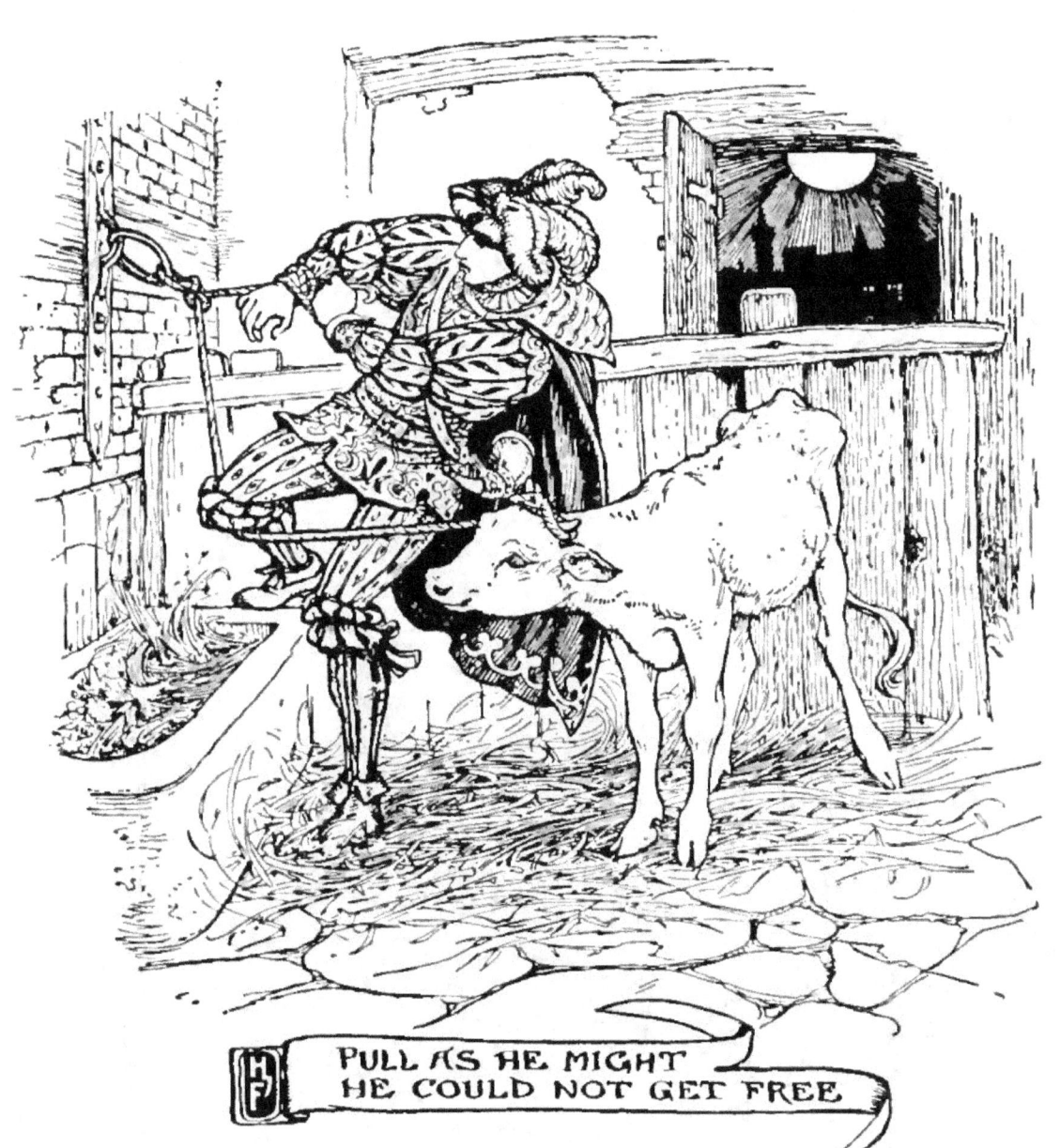

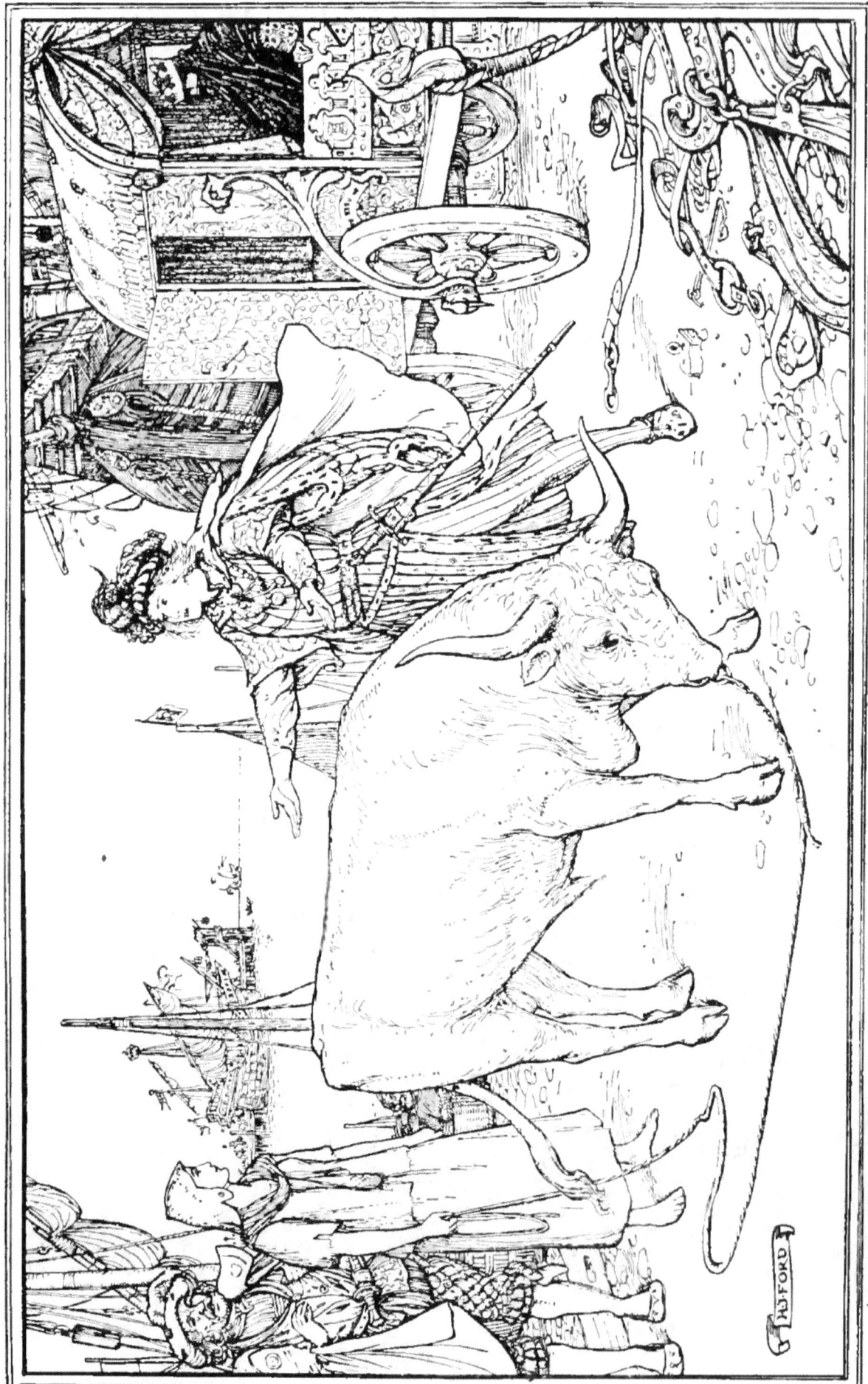

'WILL YOU LEND ME YOUR OX, FAIR MAIDEN?'

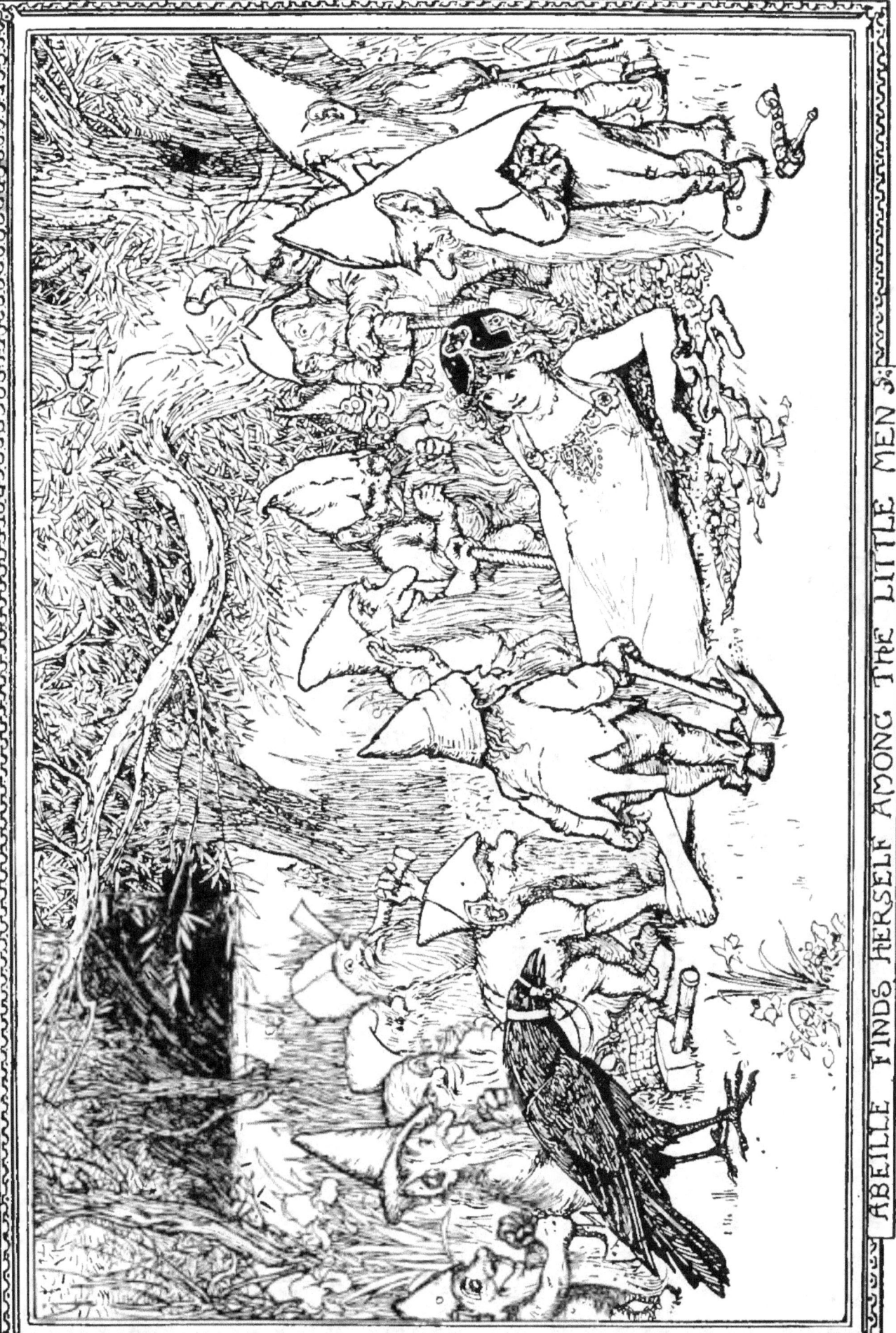
ABEILLE FINDS HERSELF AMONG THE LITTLE MEN.

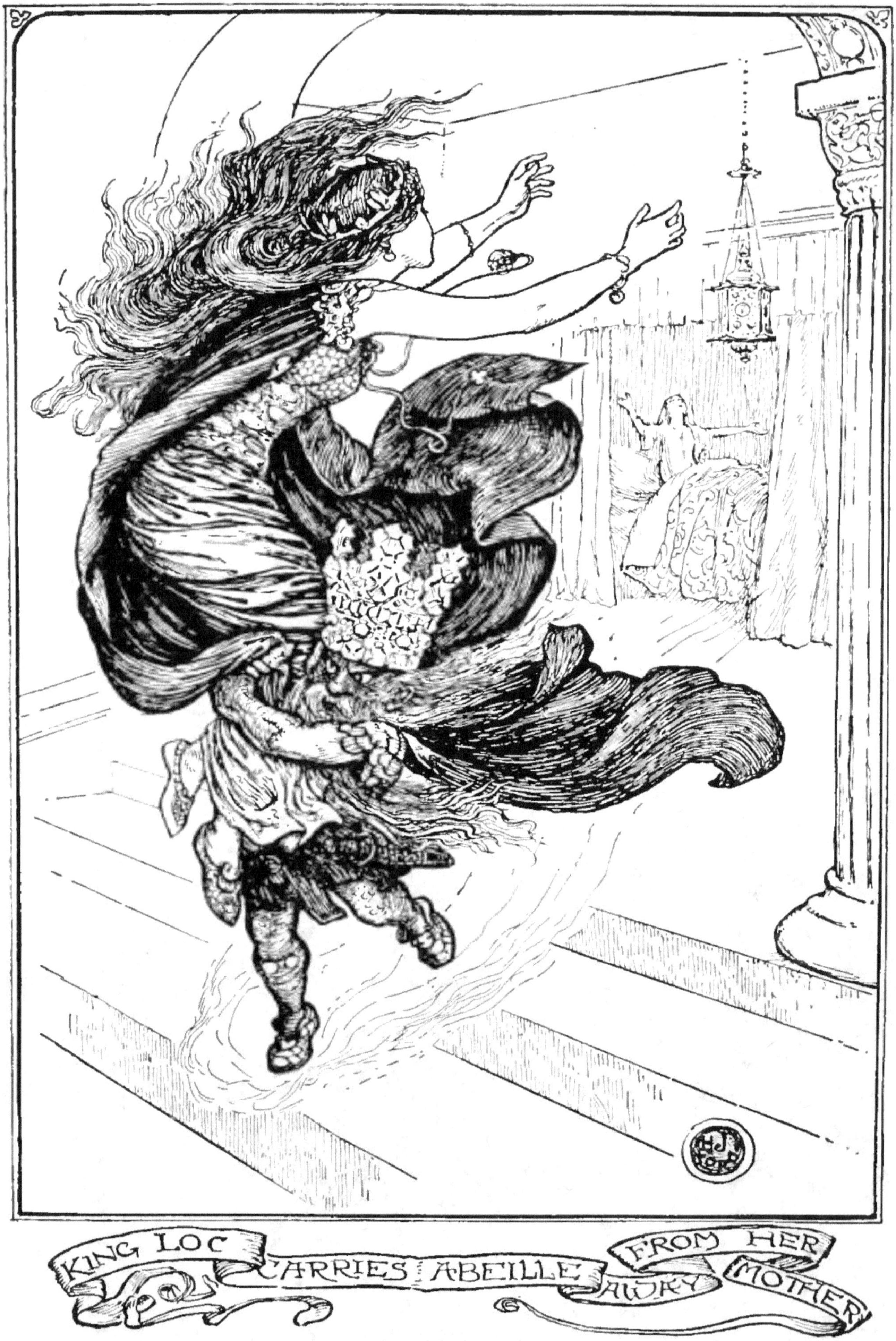

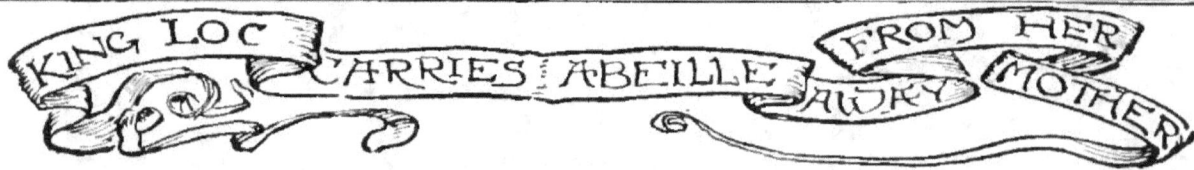
KING LOC CARRIES ABEILLE AWAY FROM HER MOTHER

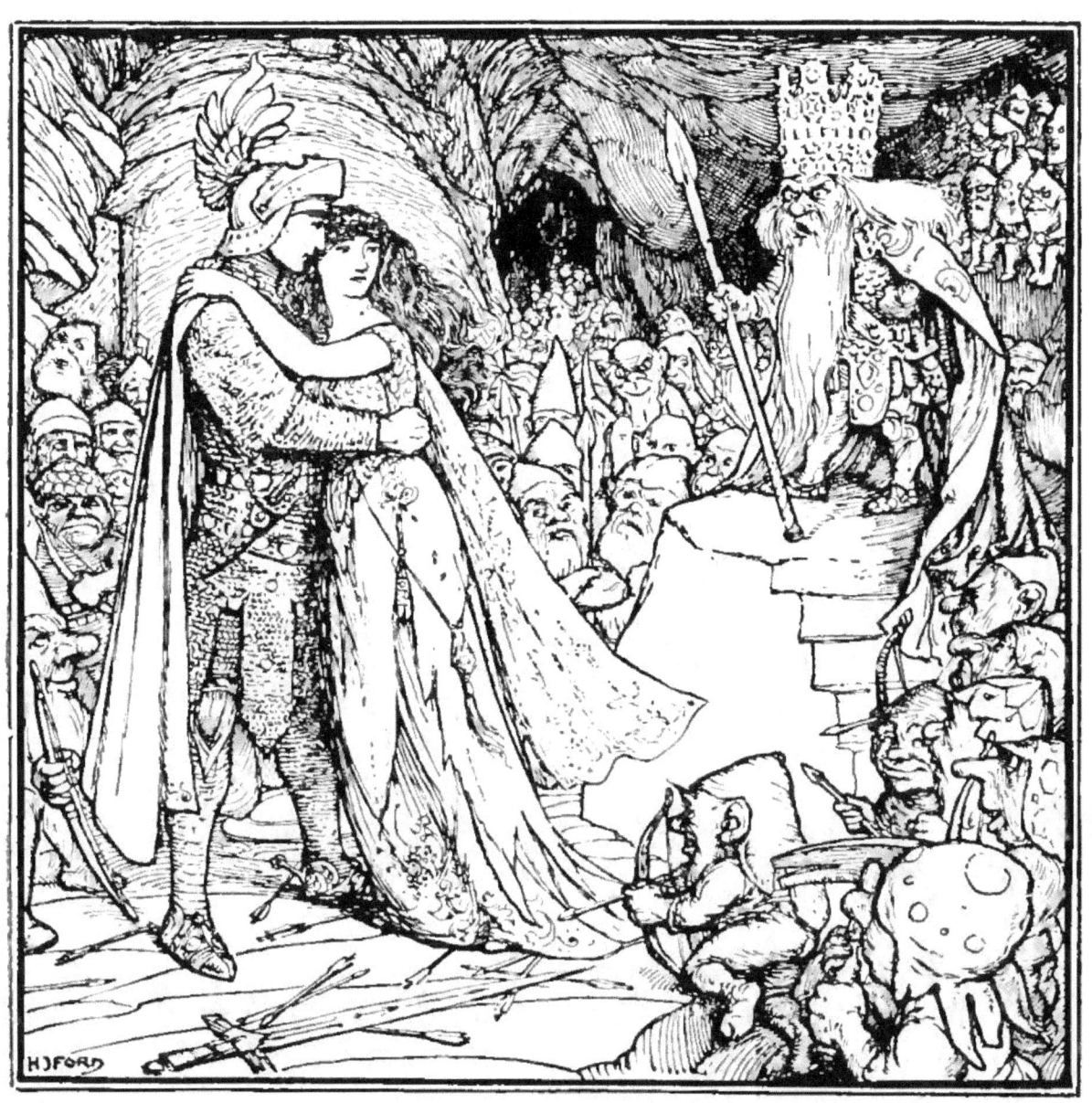
'IS THIS THE MAN THAT YOU WISH TO MARRY?'

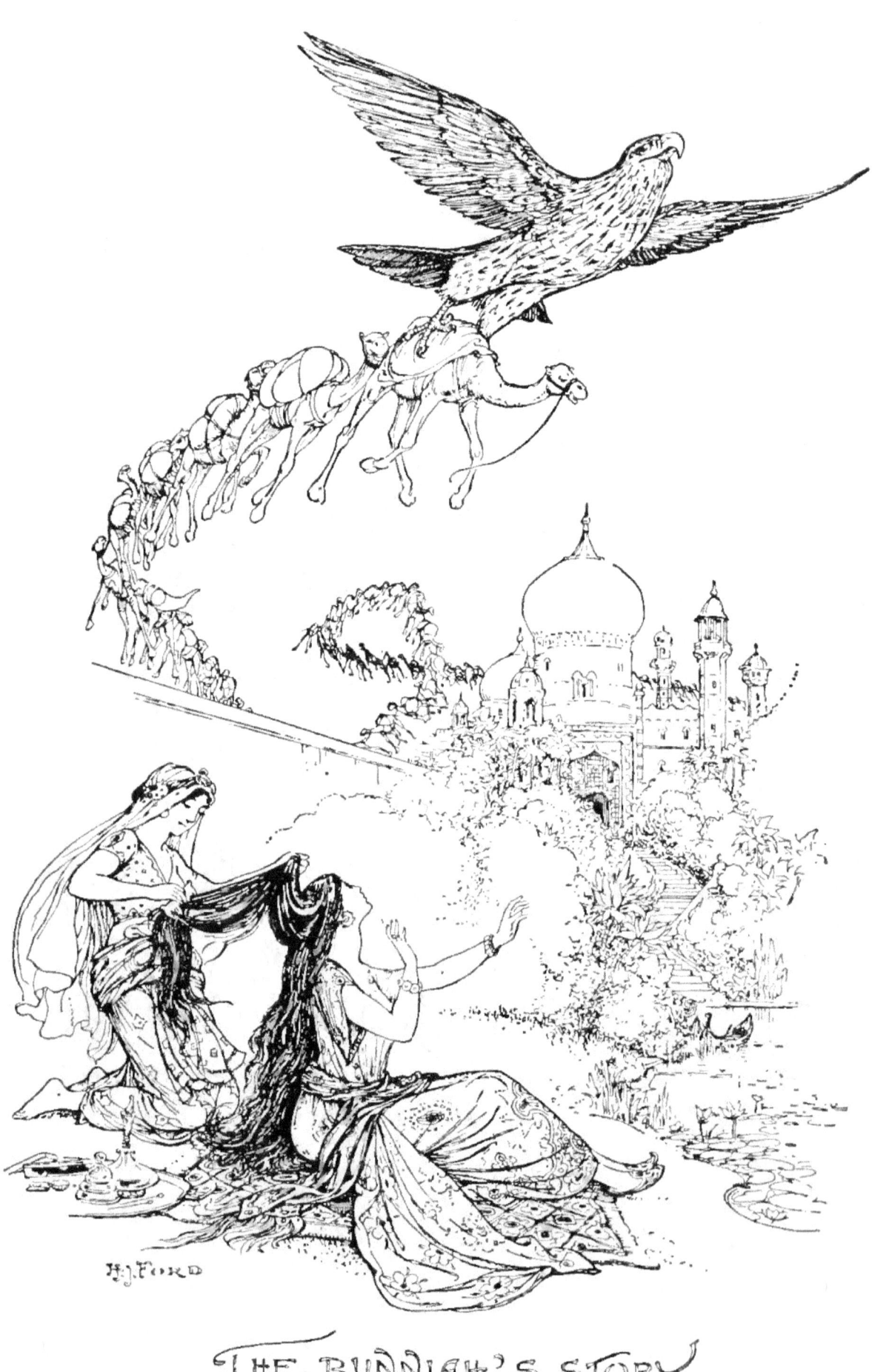
THE BUNNIAH'S STORY

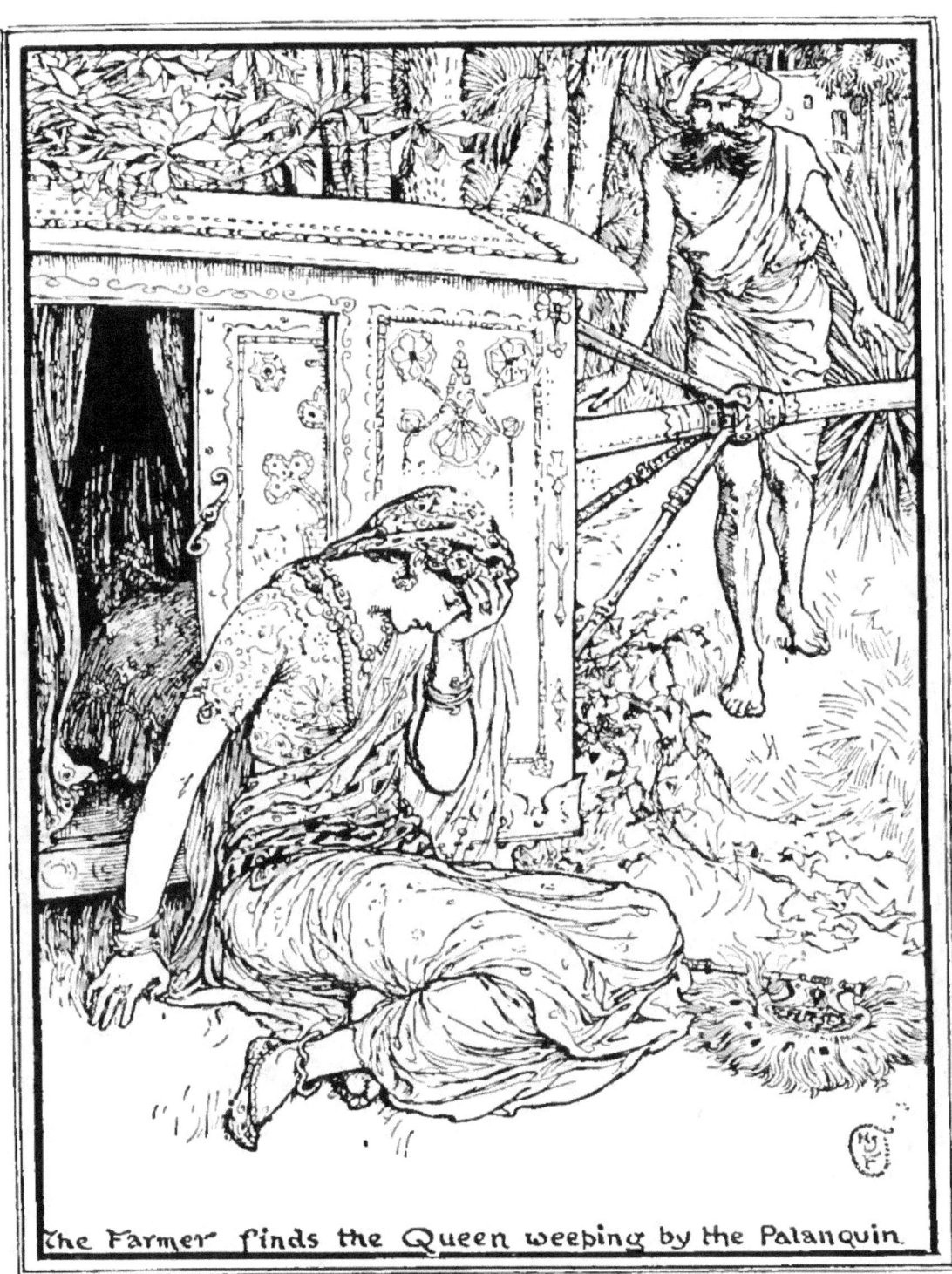

The Farmer finds the Queen weeping by the Palanquin.

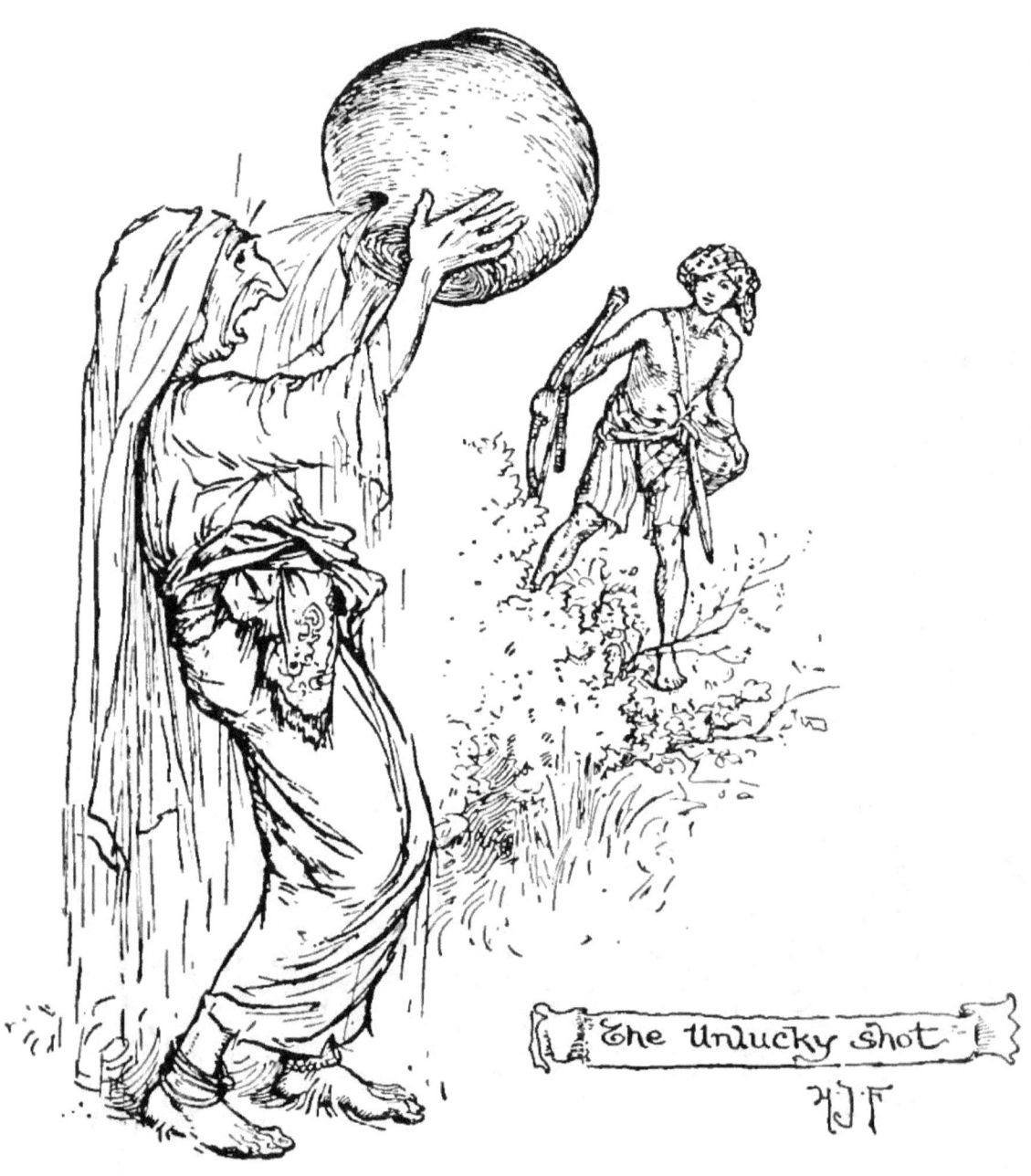

The Unlucky Shot

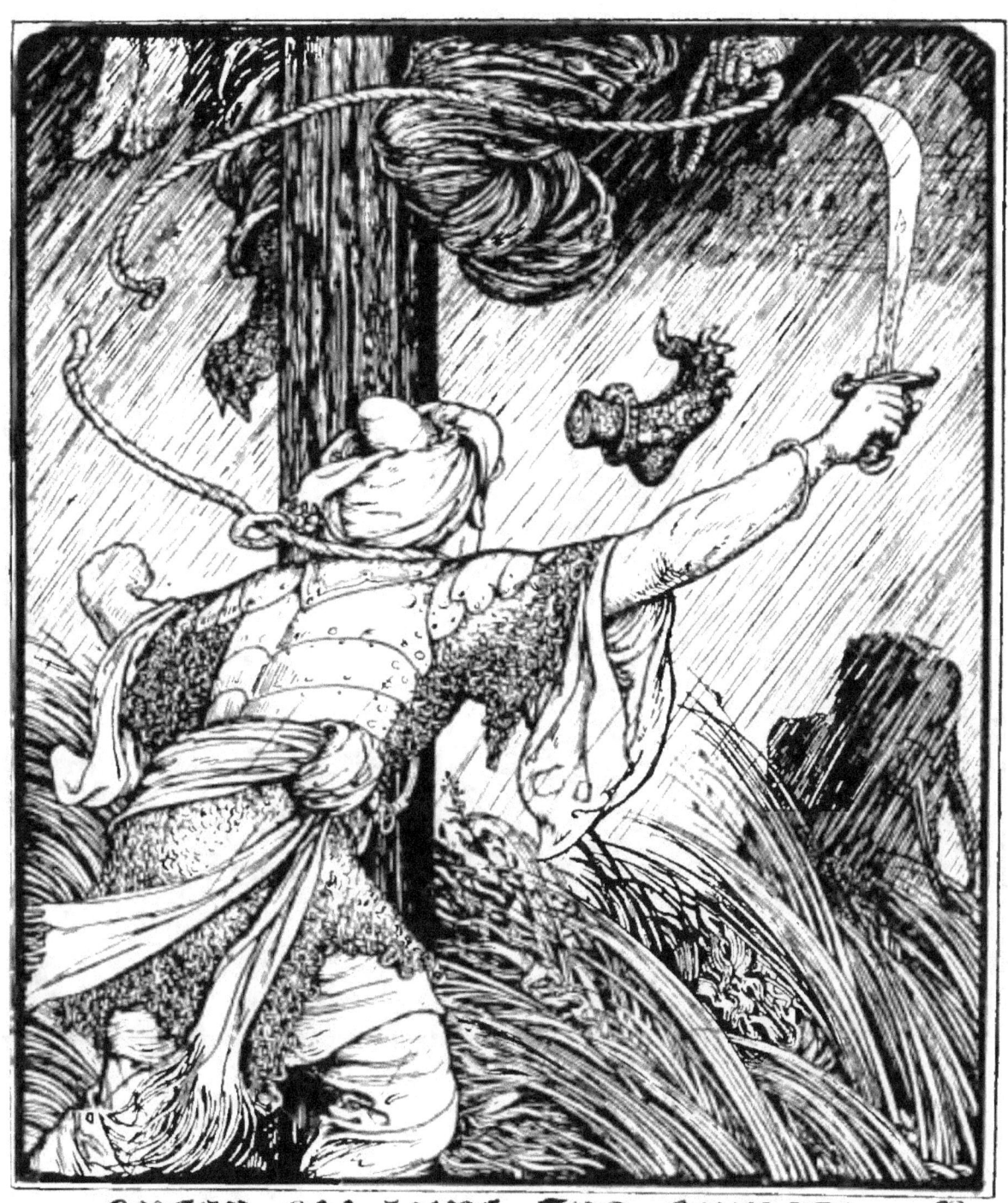

AMEER ALI WINS THE ANKLET

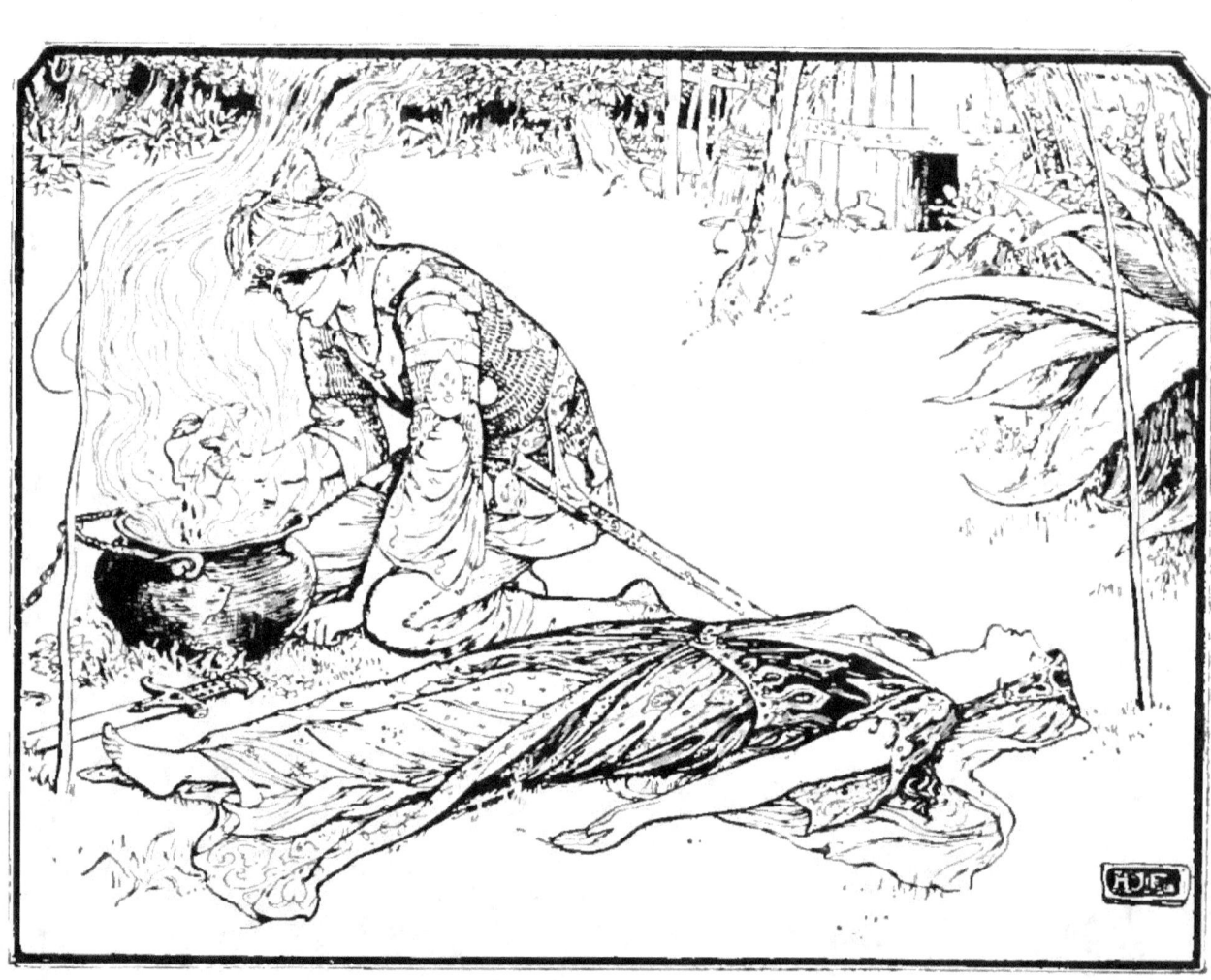

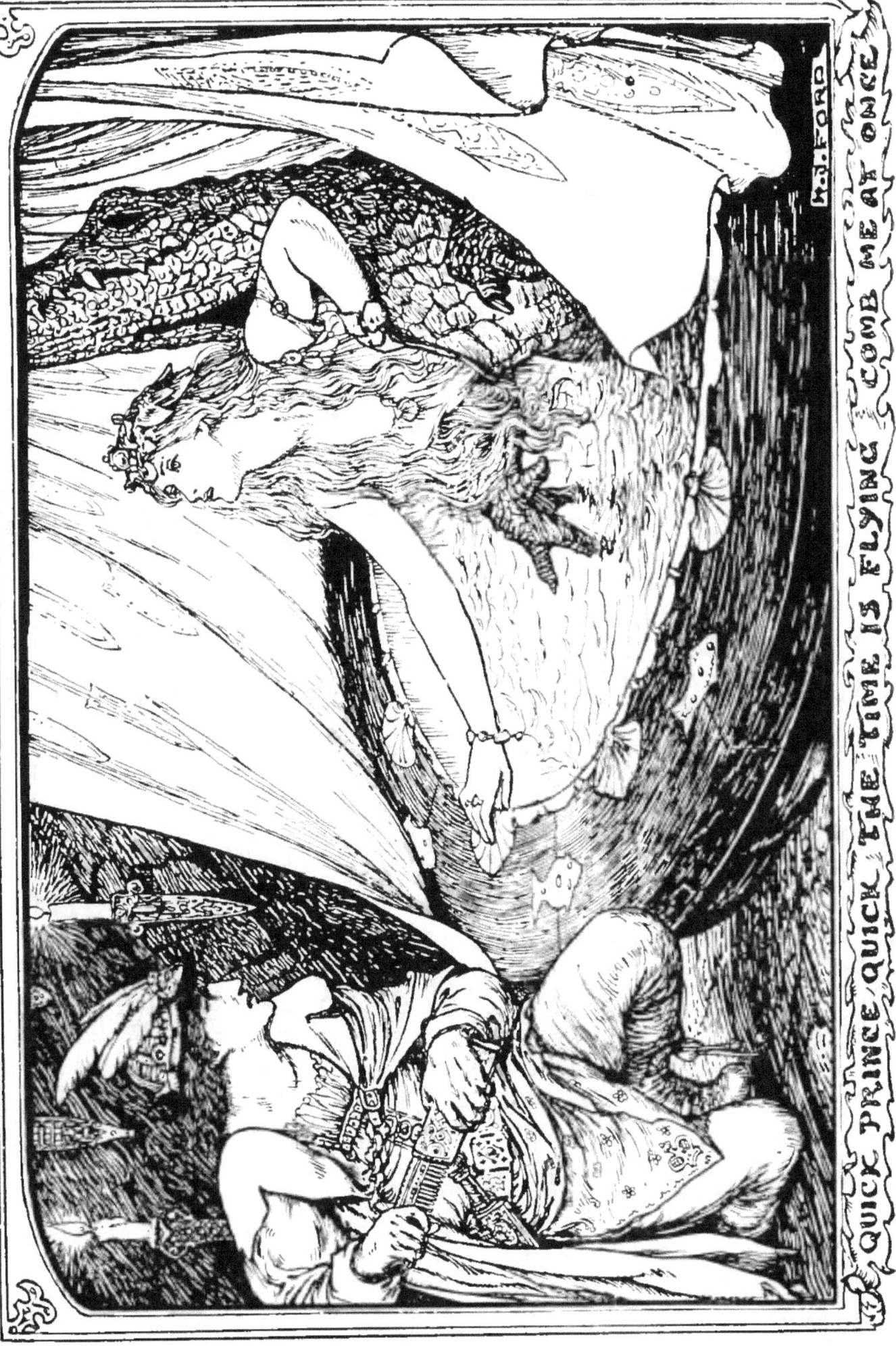

QUICK PRINCE QUICK THE TIME IS FLYING COMB ME AT ONCE

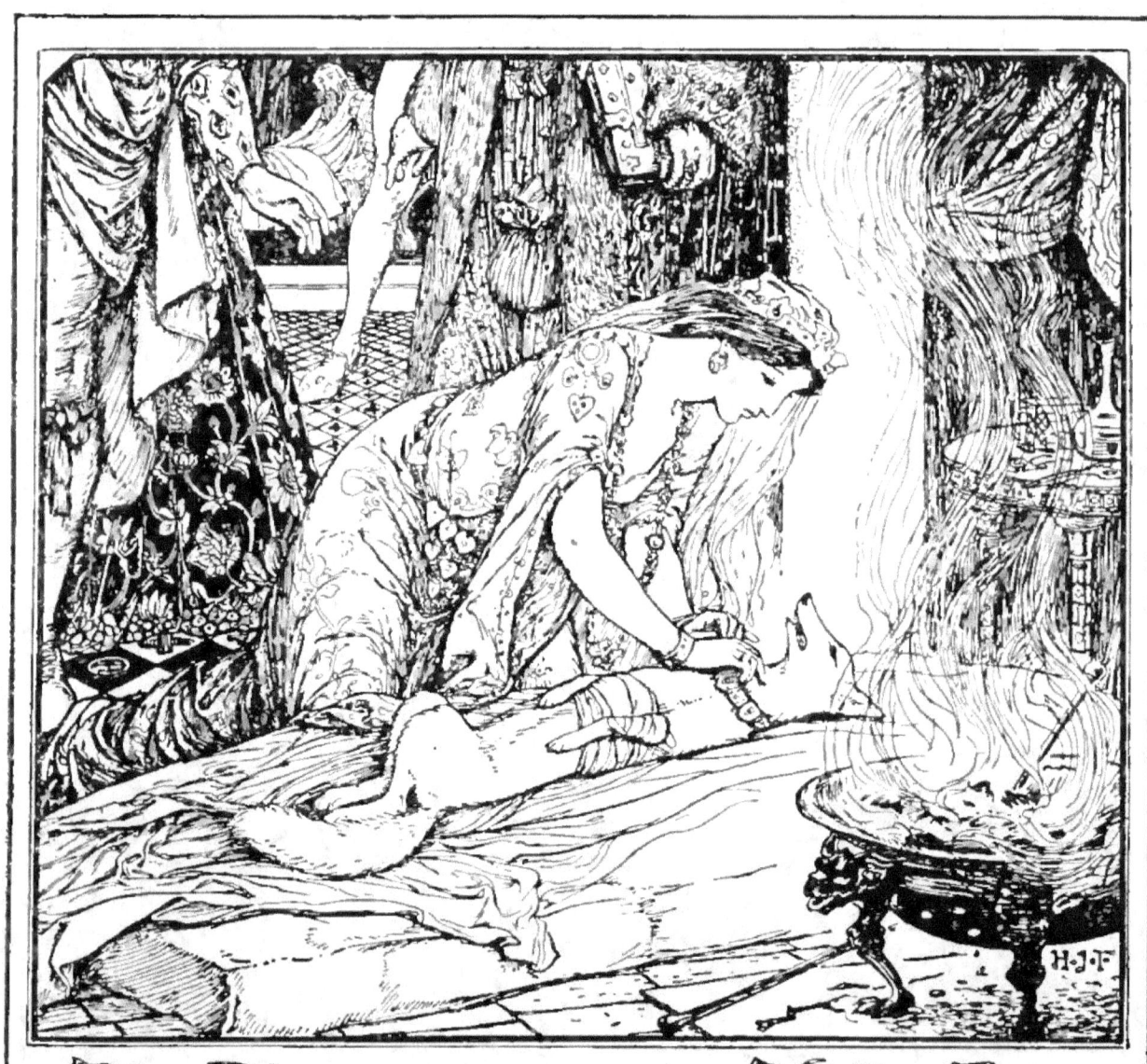
The Princess saves the White Fox

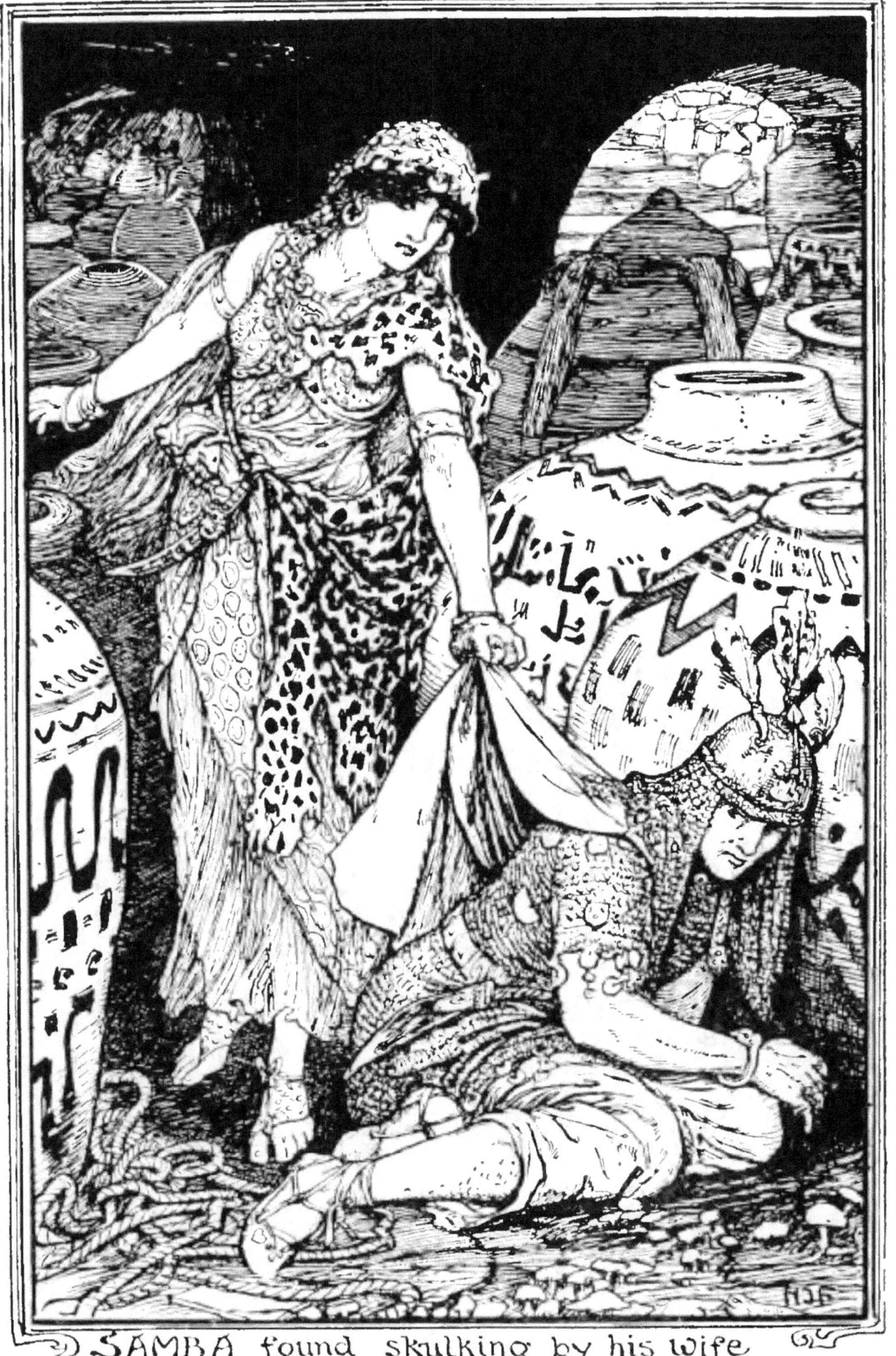
SAMBA found skulking by his wife

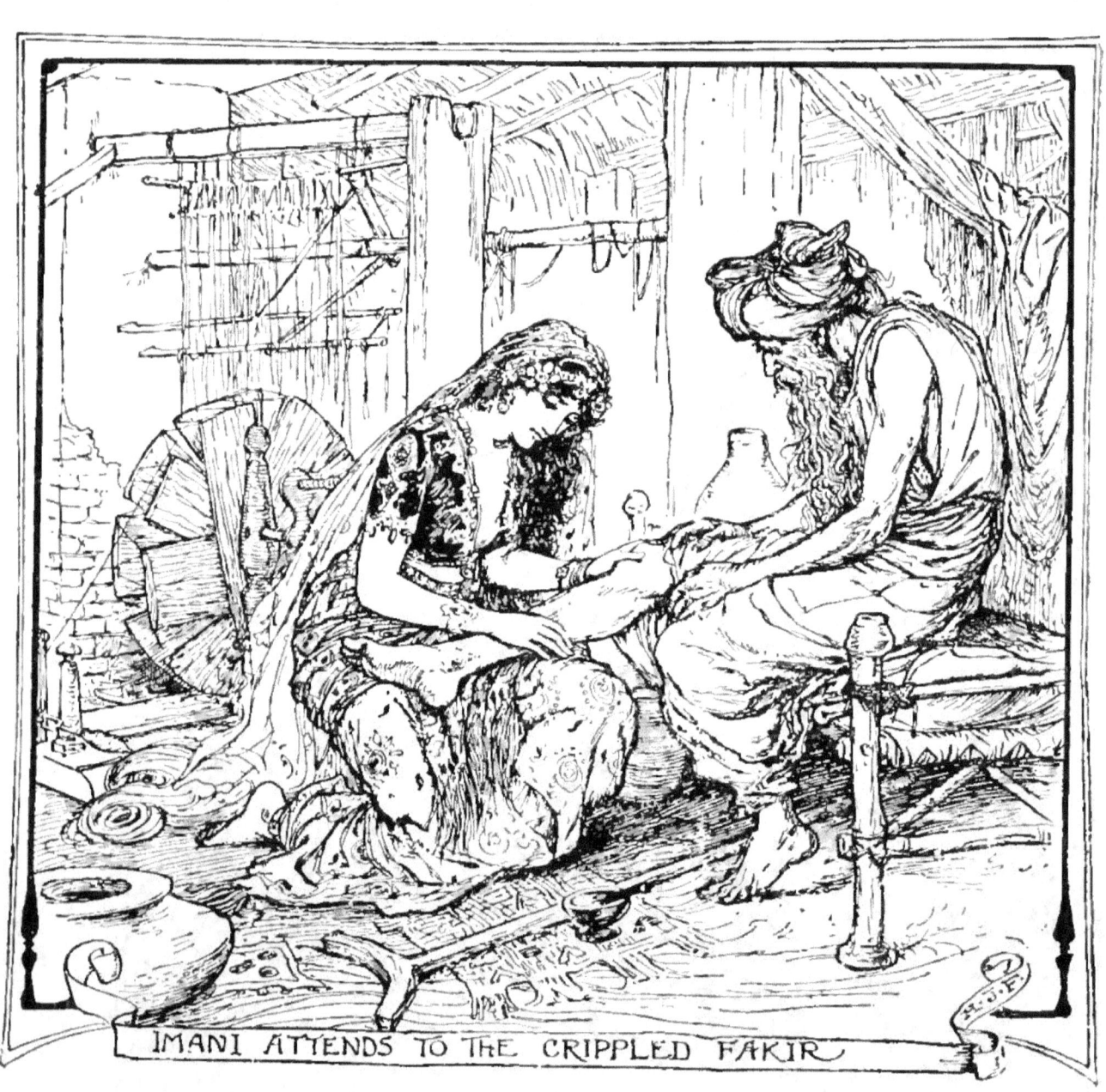
IMANI ATTENDS TO THE CRIPPLED FAKIR

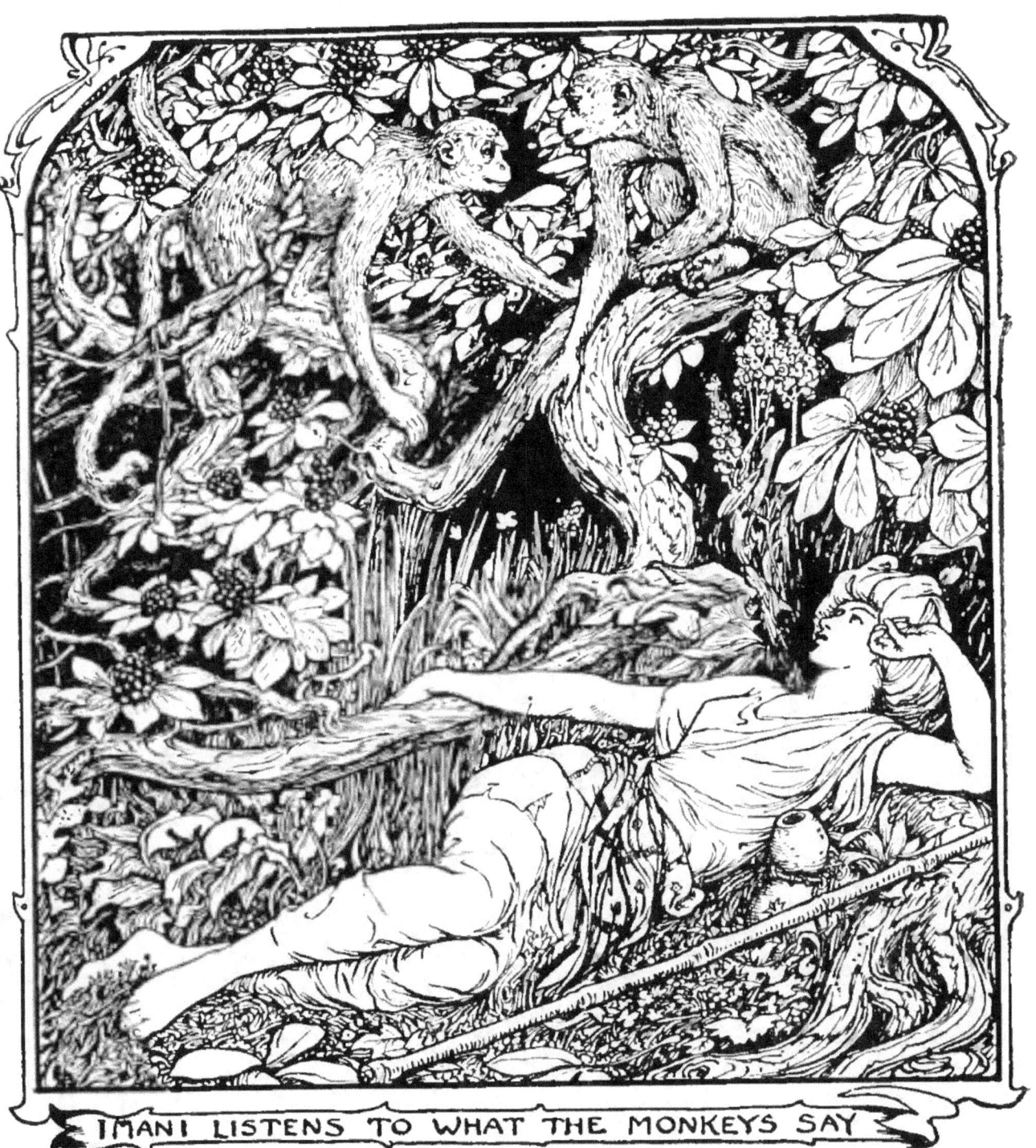
IMANI LISTENS TO WHAT THE MONKEYS SAY

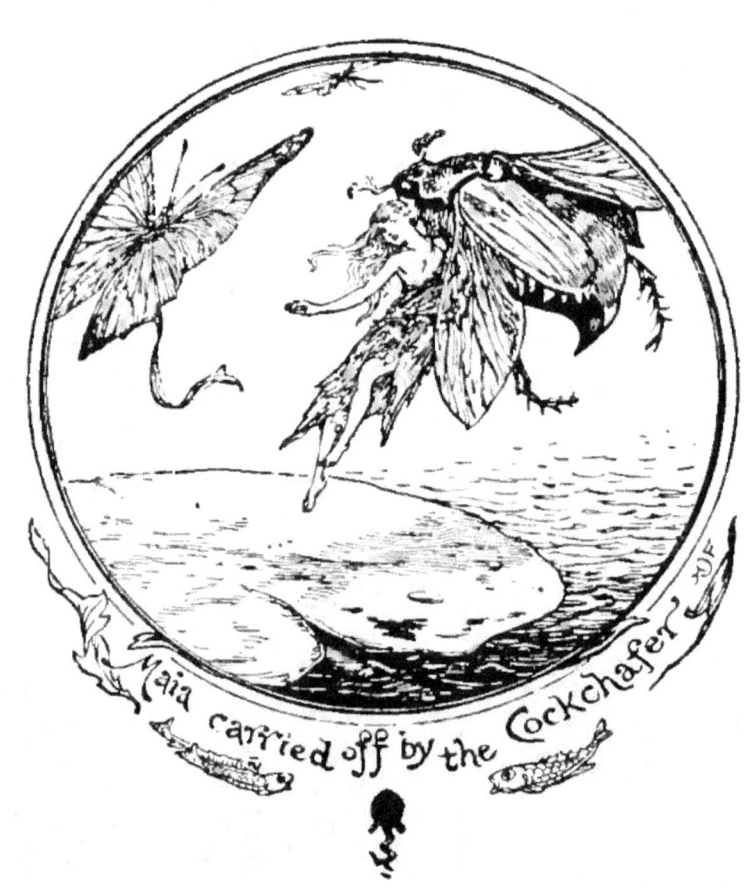

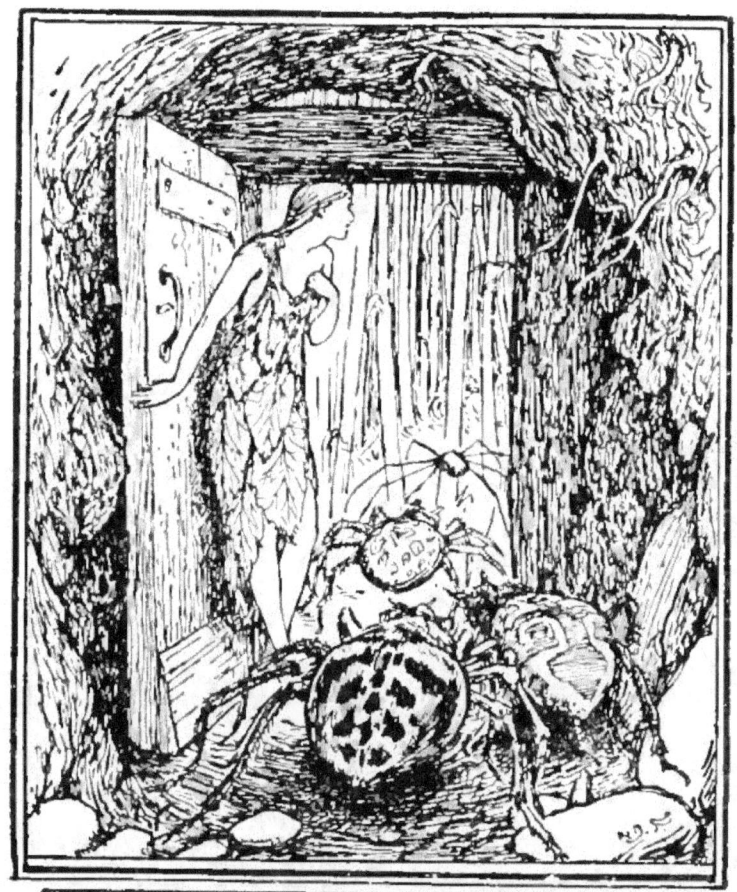
MAIA AND THE SPIDERS IN THE EVENING

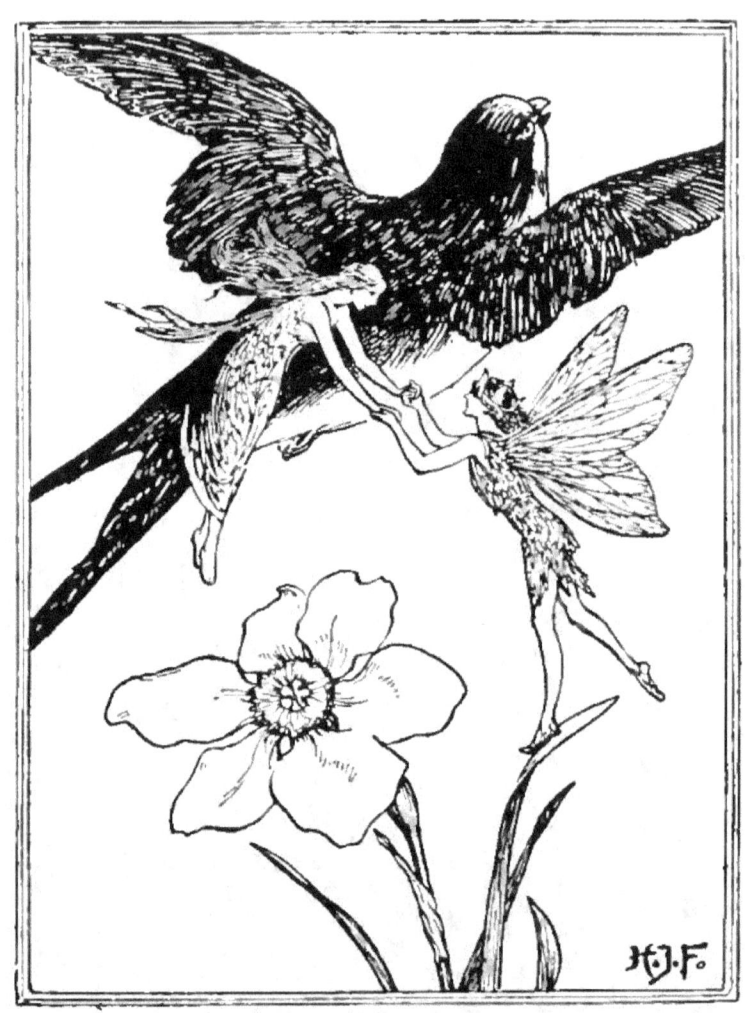

He helped her to jump from the Swallow's back

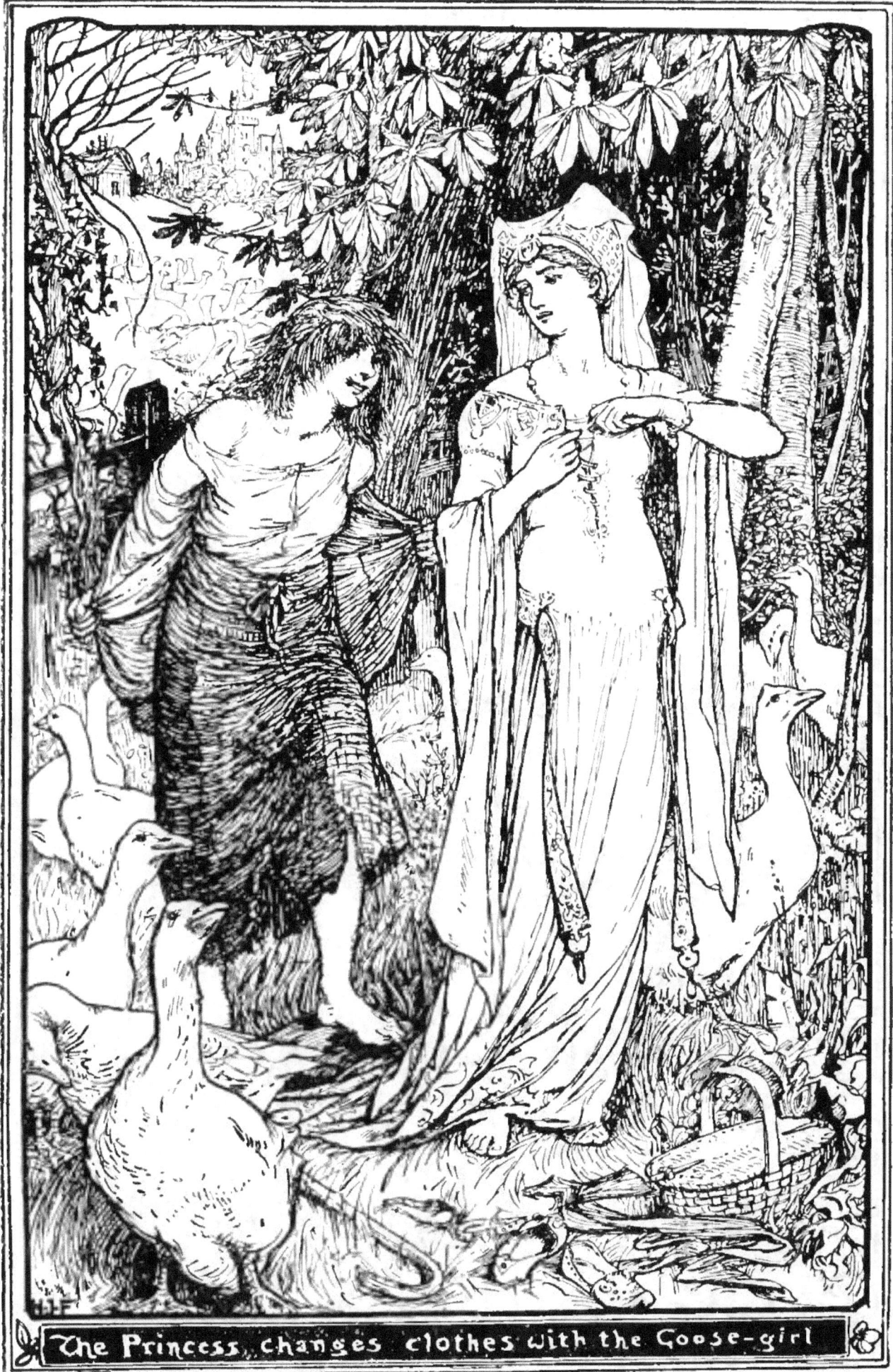
The Princess changes clothes with the Goose-girl

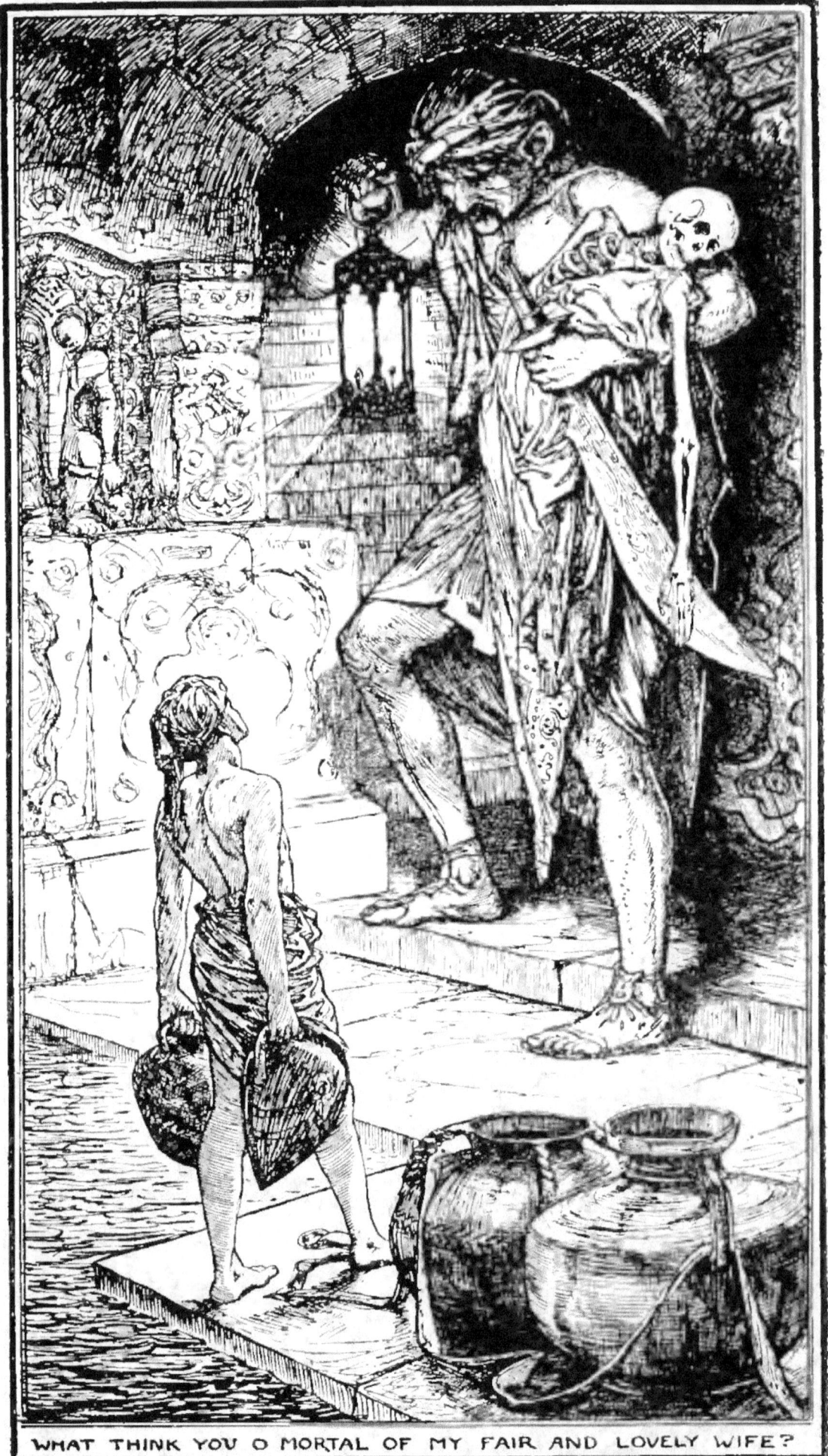
WHAT THINK YOU O MORTAL OF MY FAIR AND LOVELY WIFE?

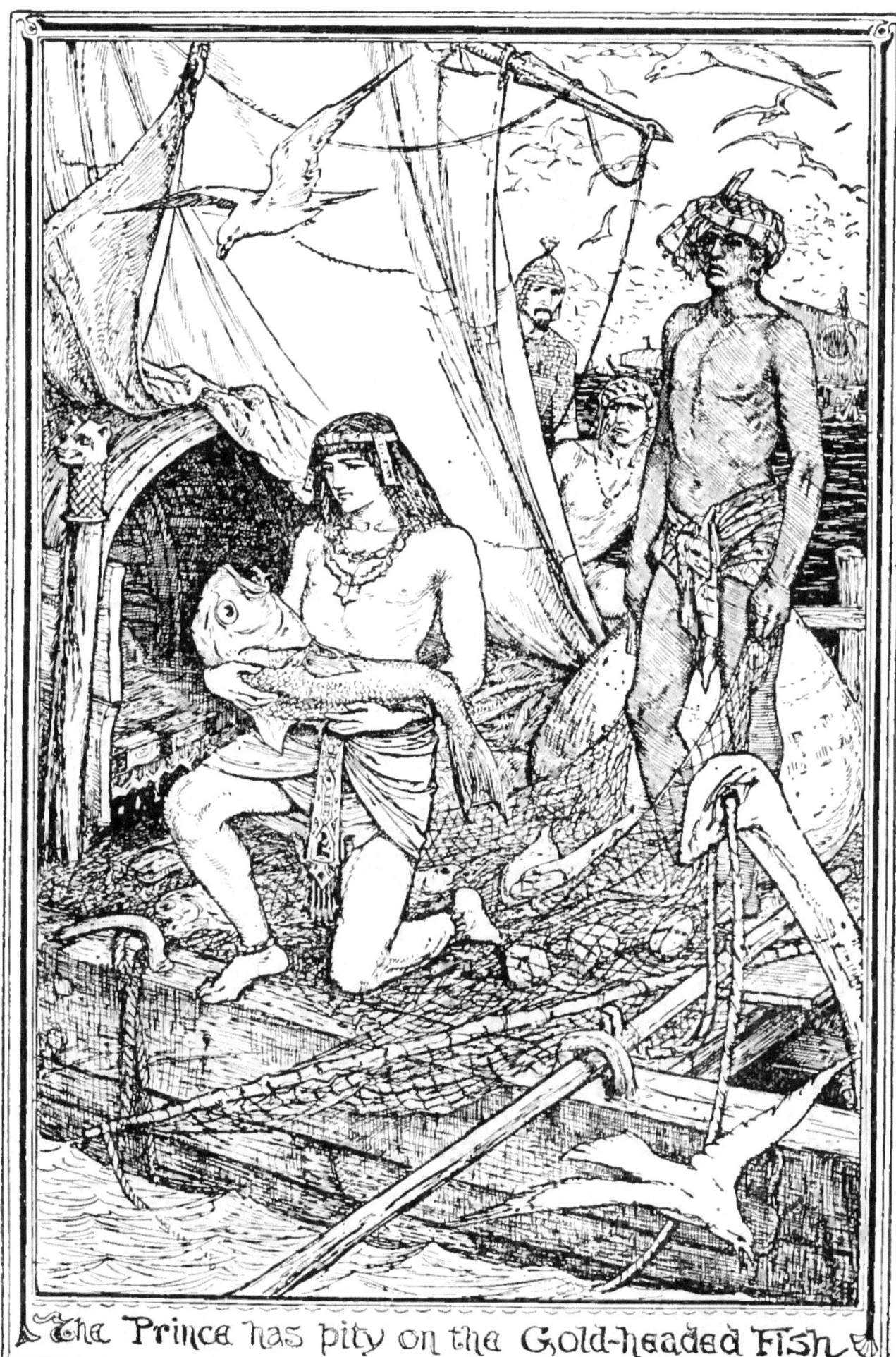
The Prince has pity on the Gold-headed Fish

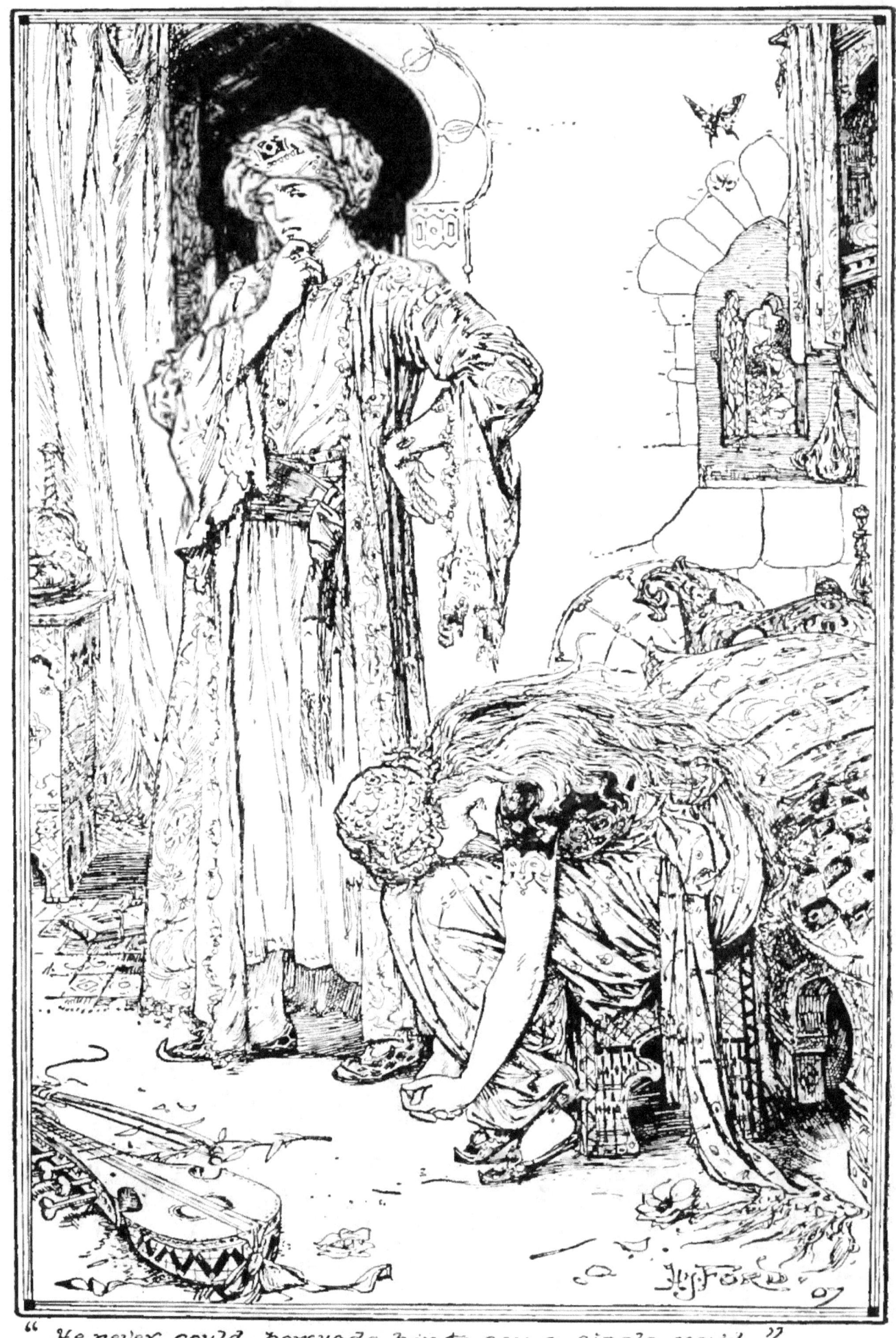

"He never could persuade her to say a single word"

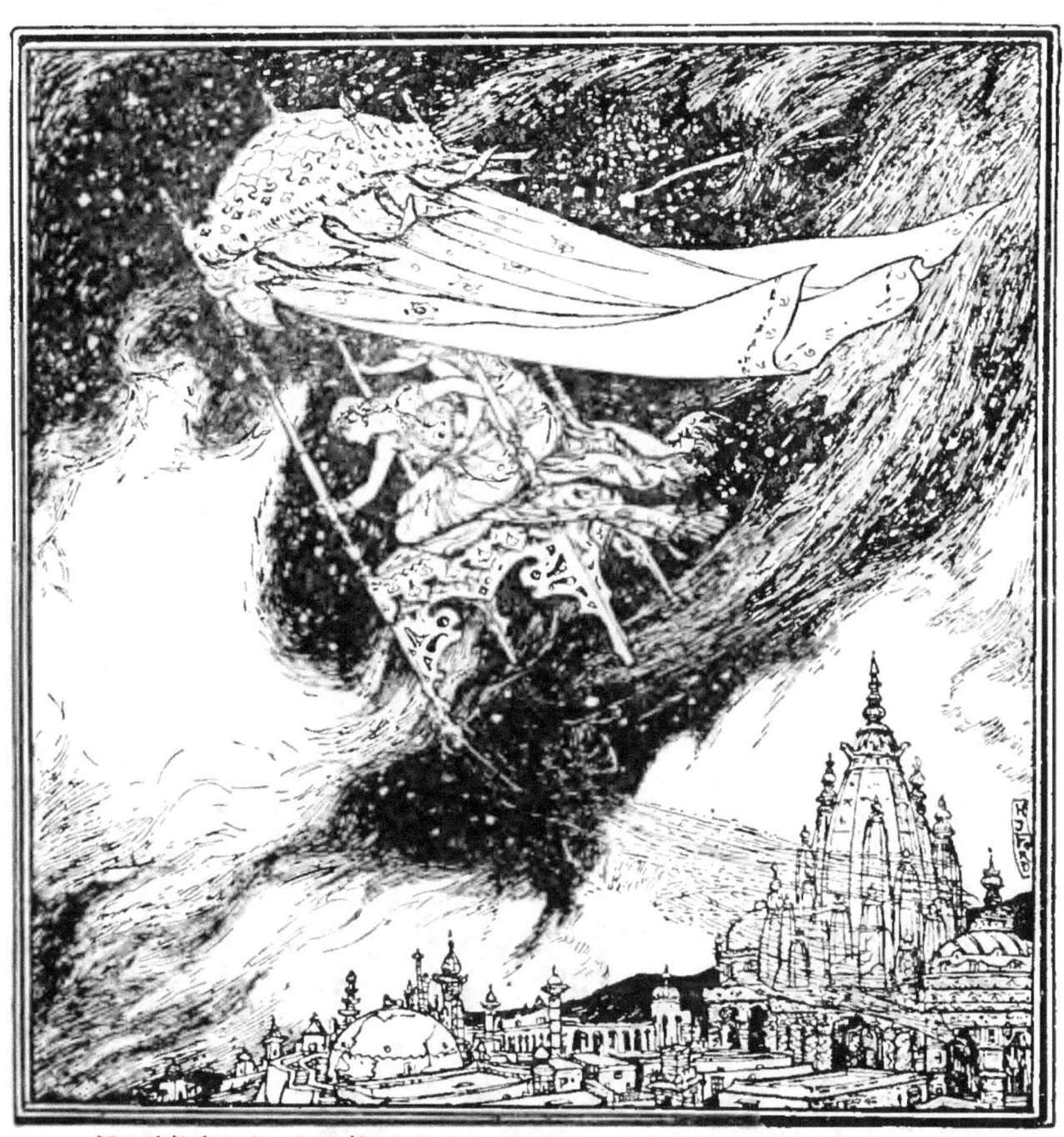
THE INVISIBLE PRINCE GOES WITH THE LADIES

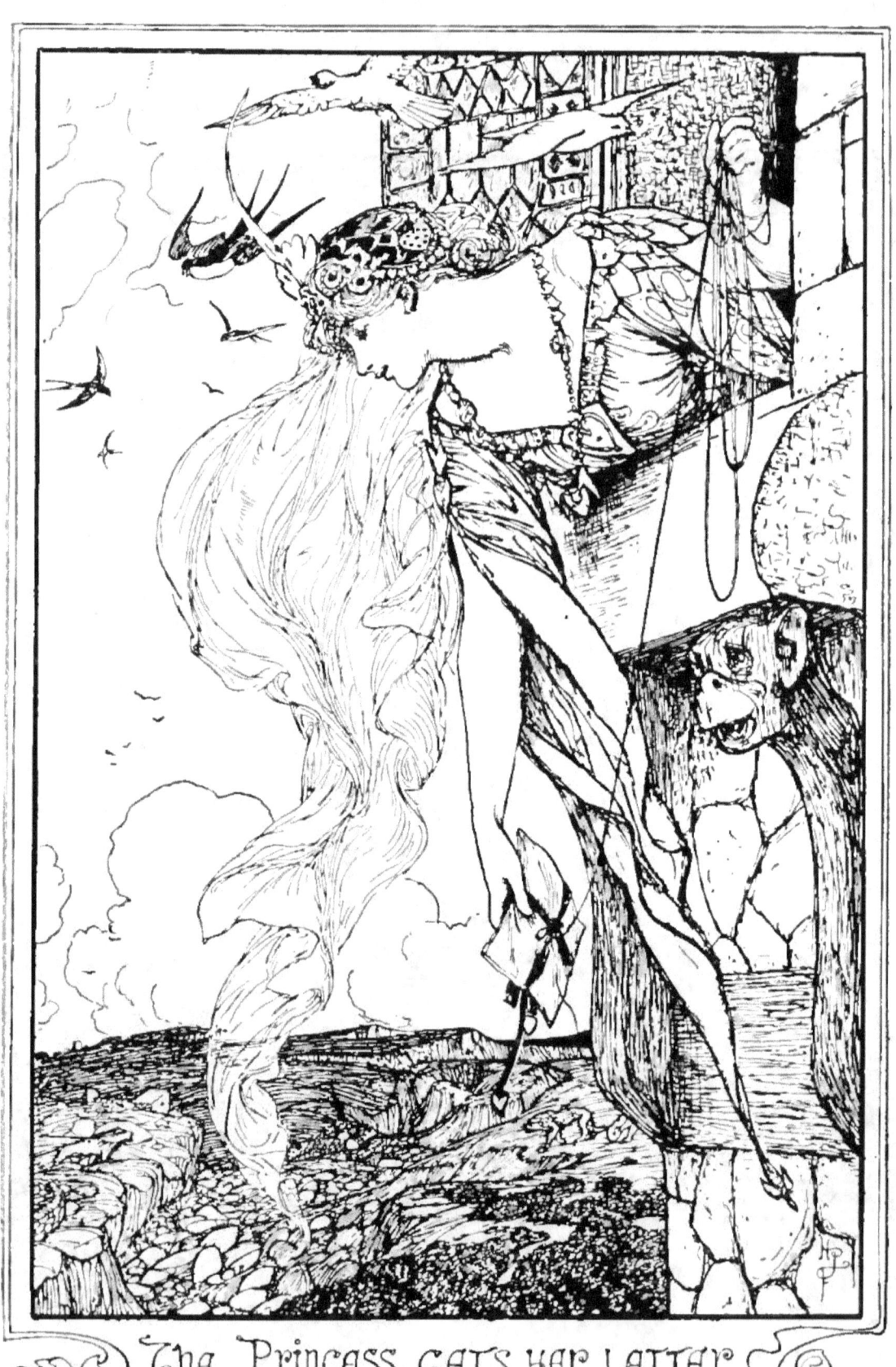
The Princess Gets Her Letter

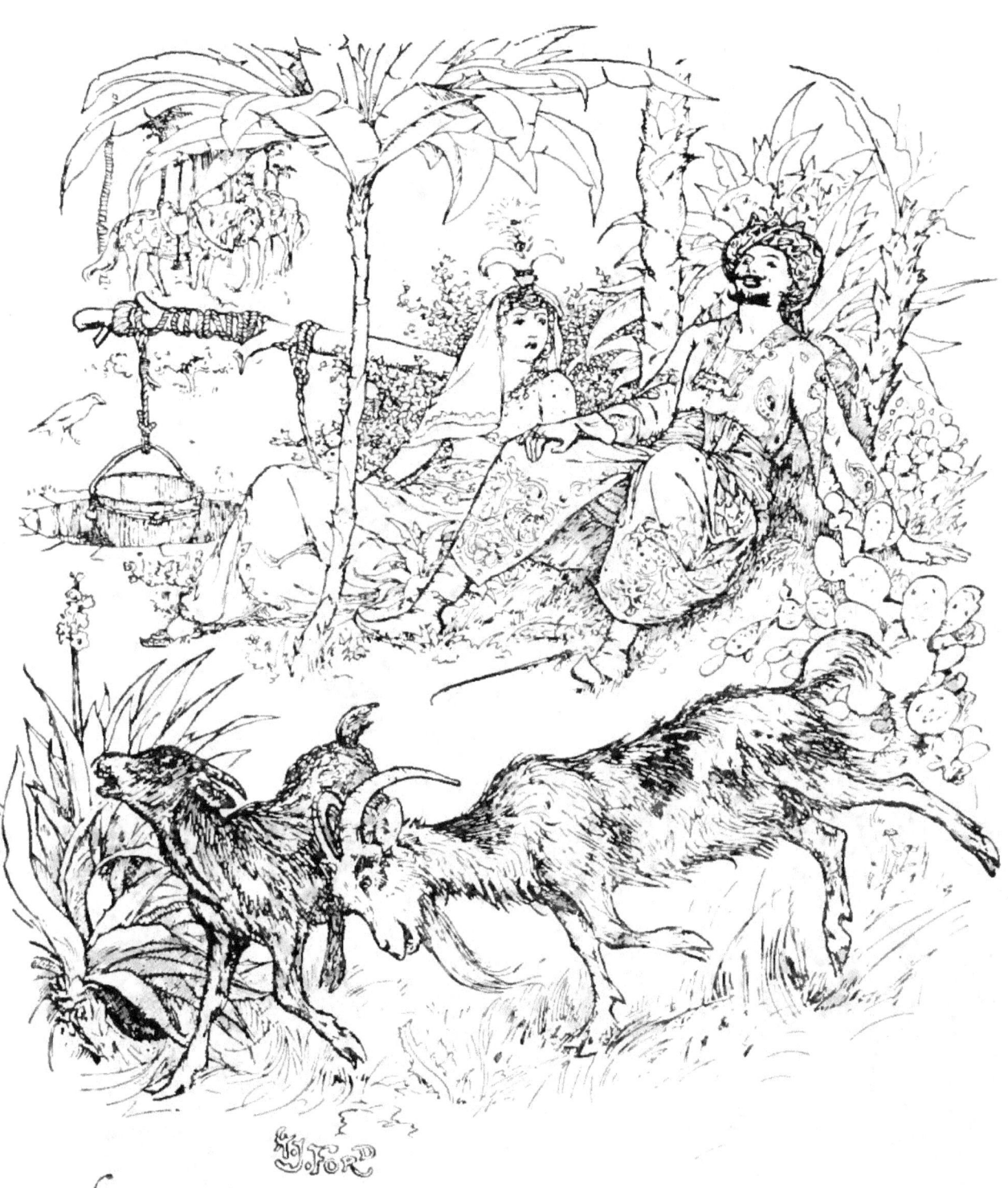

The King laughs at the Billygoat

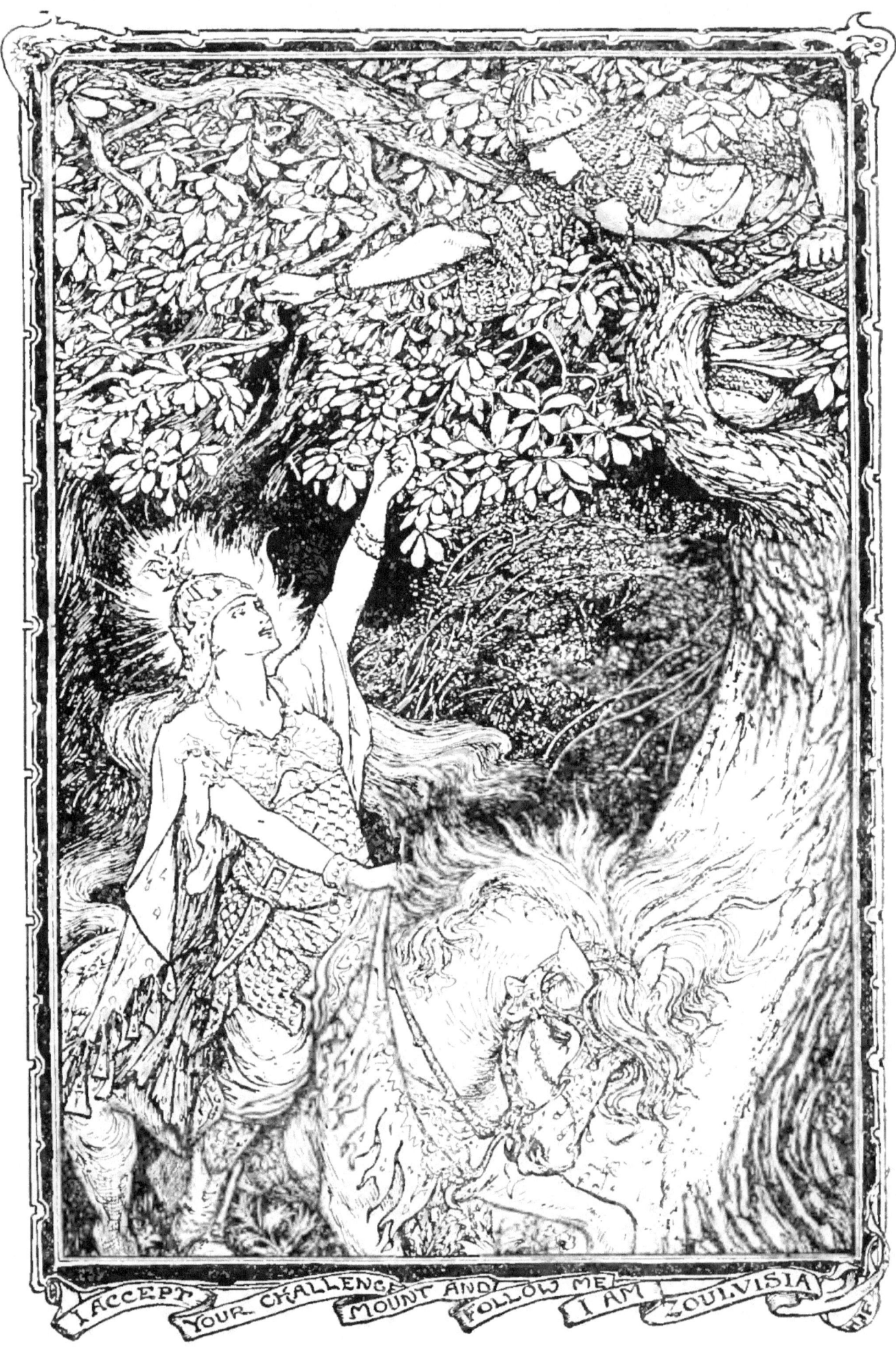
"I ACCEPT YOUR CHALLENGE MOUNT AND FOLLOW ME I AM ZOULVISIA"

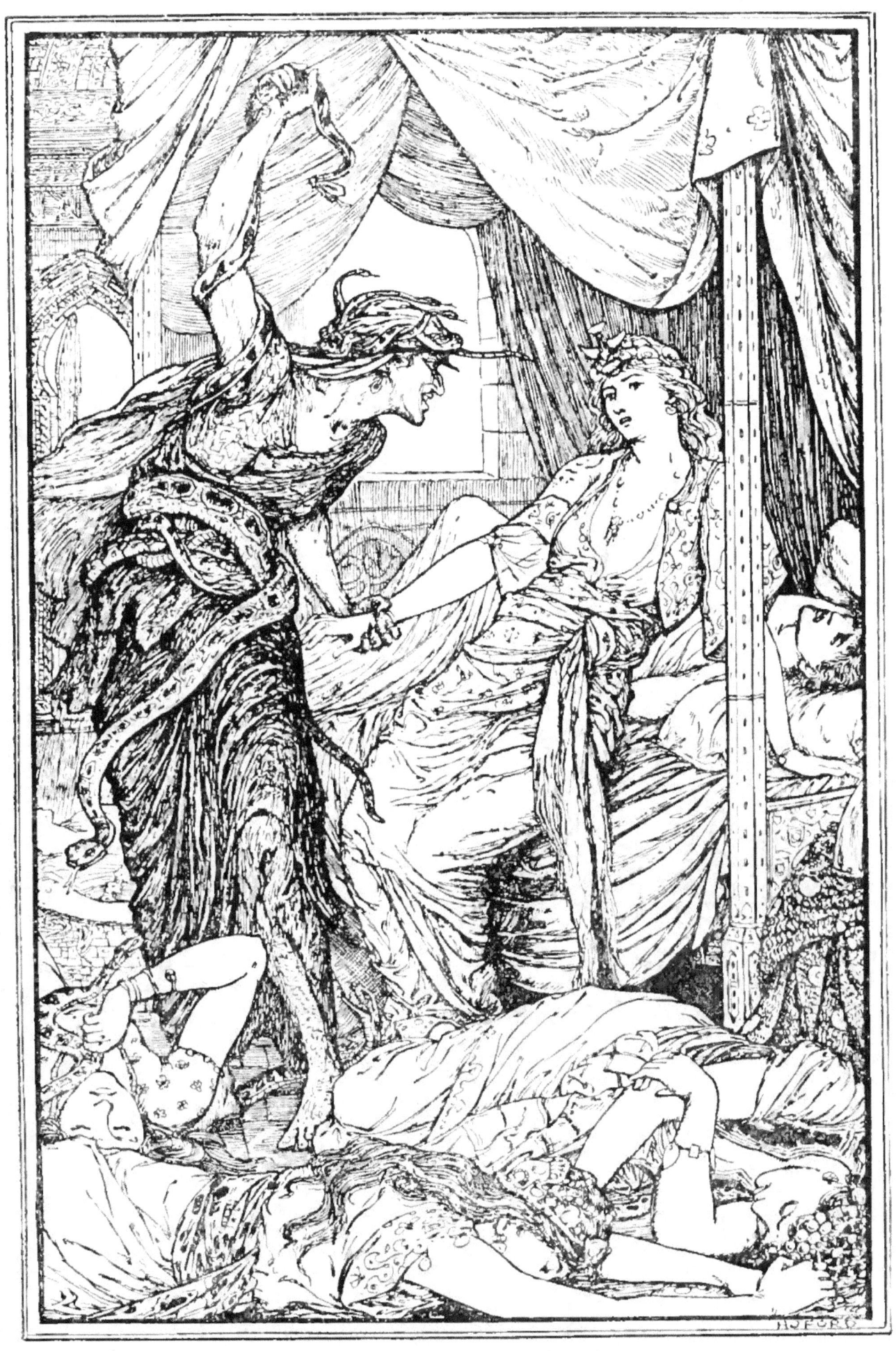
The Witch and her Snakes

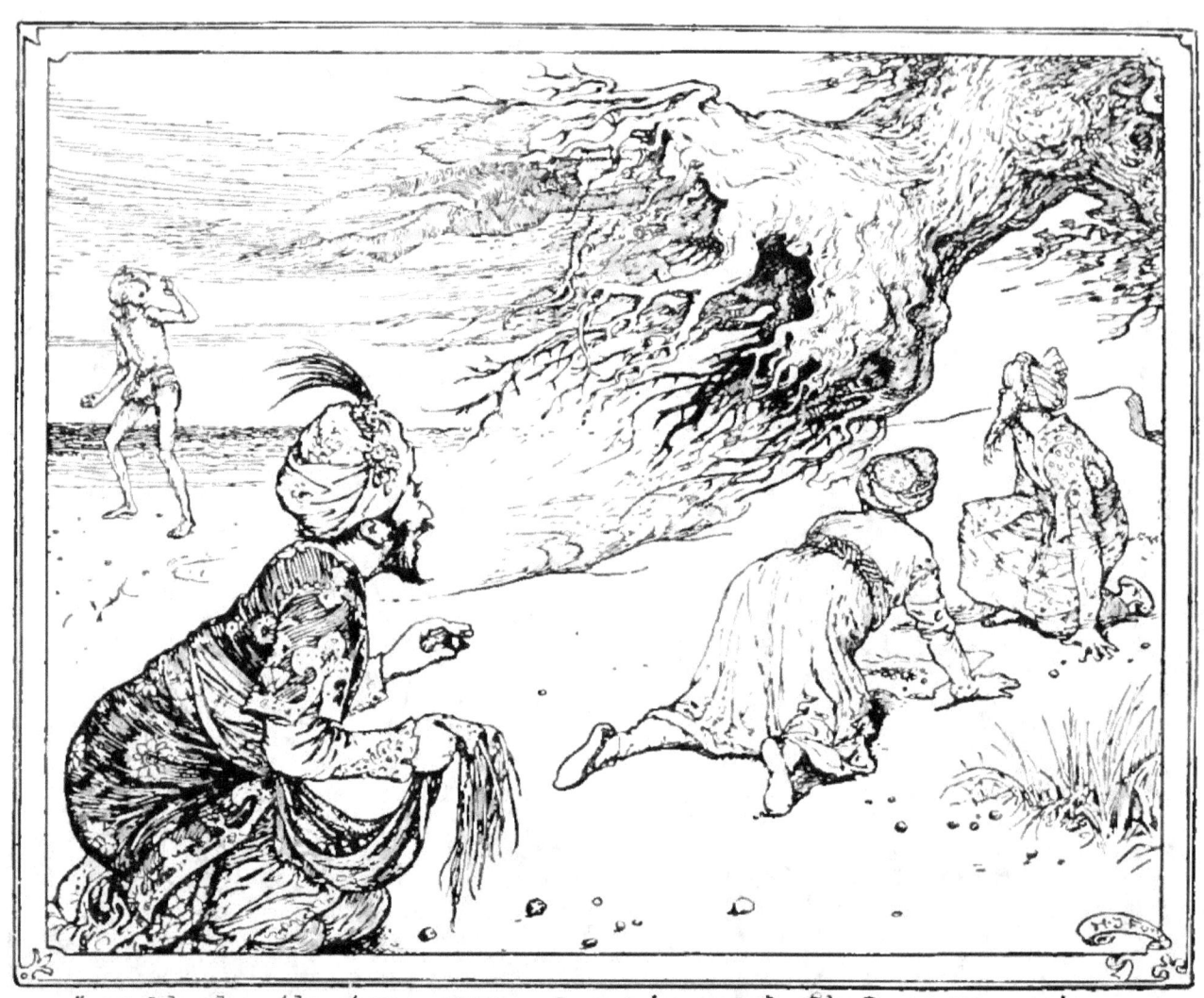
"suddenly the tree rose up again and flew away"

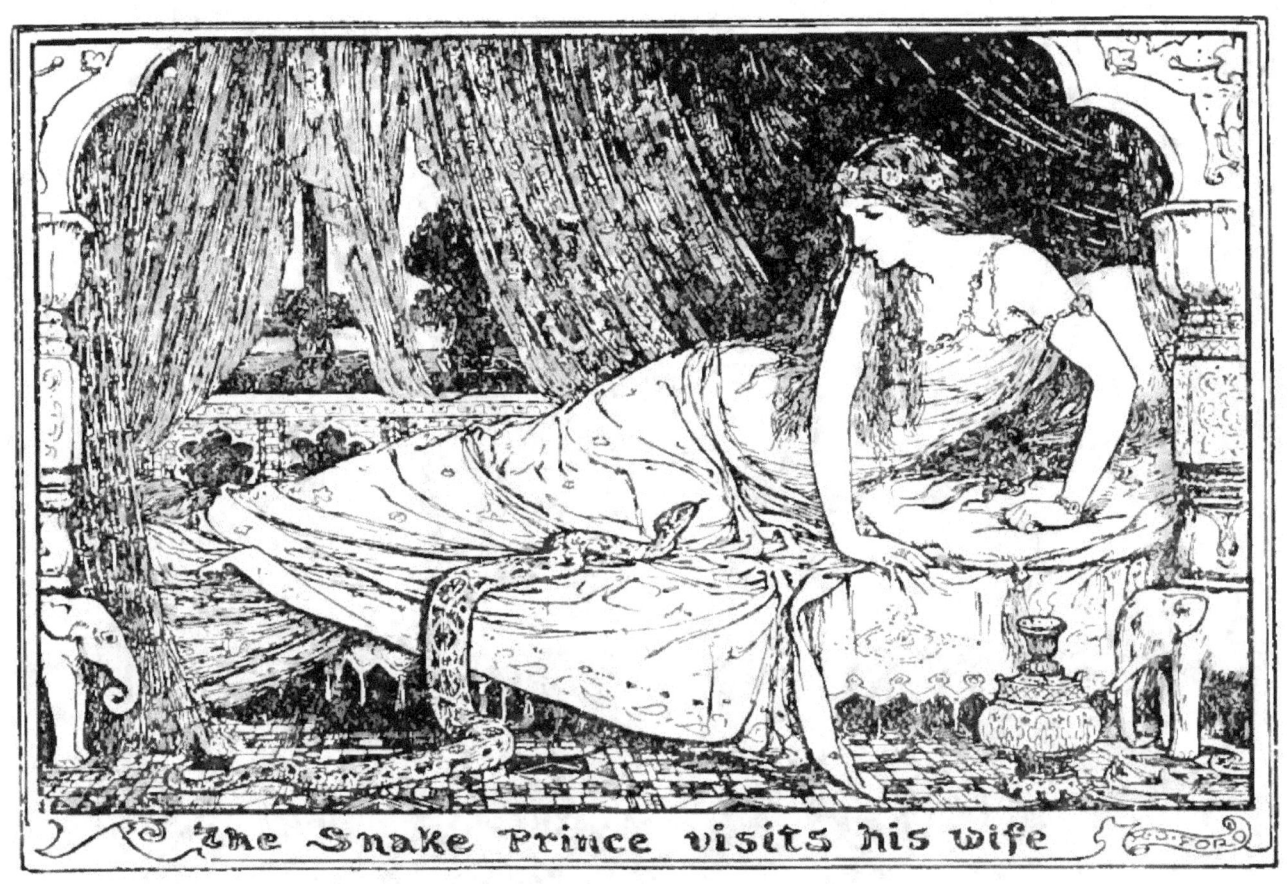
The Snake Prince visits his wife

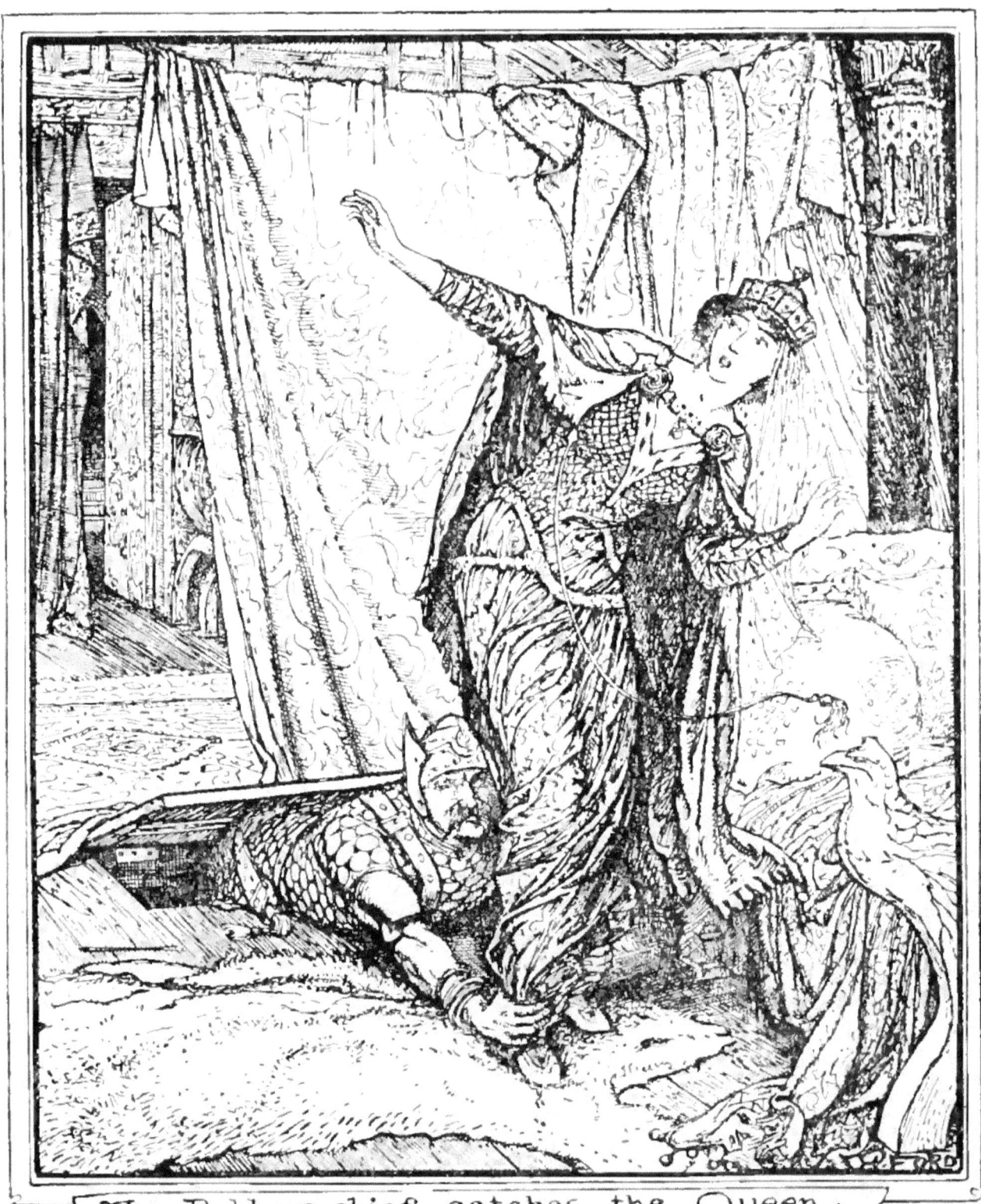
The Robber-chief catches the Queen

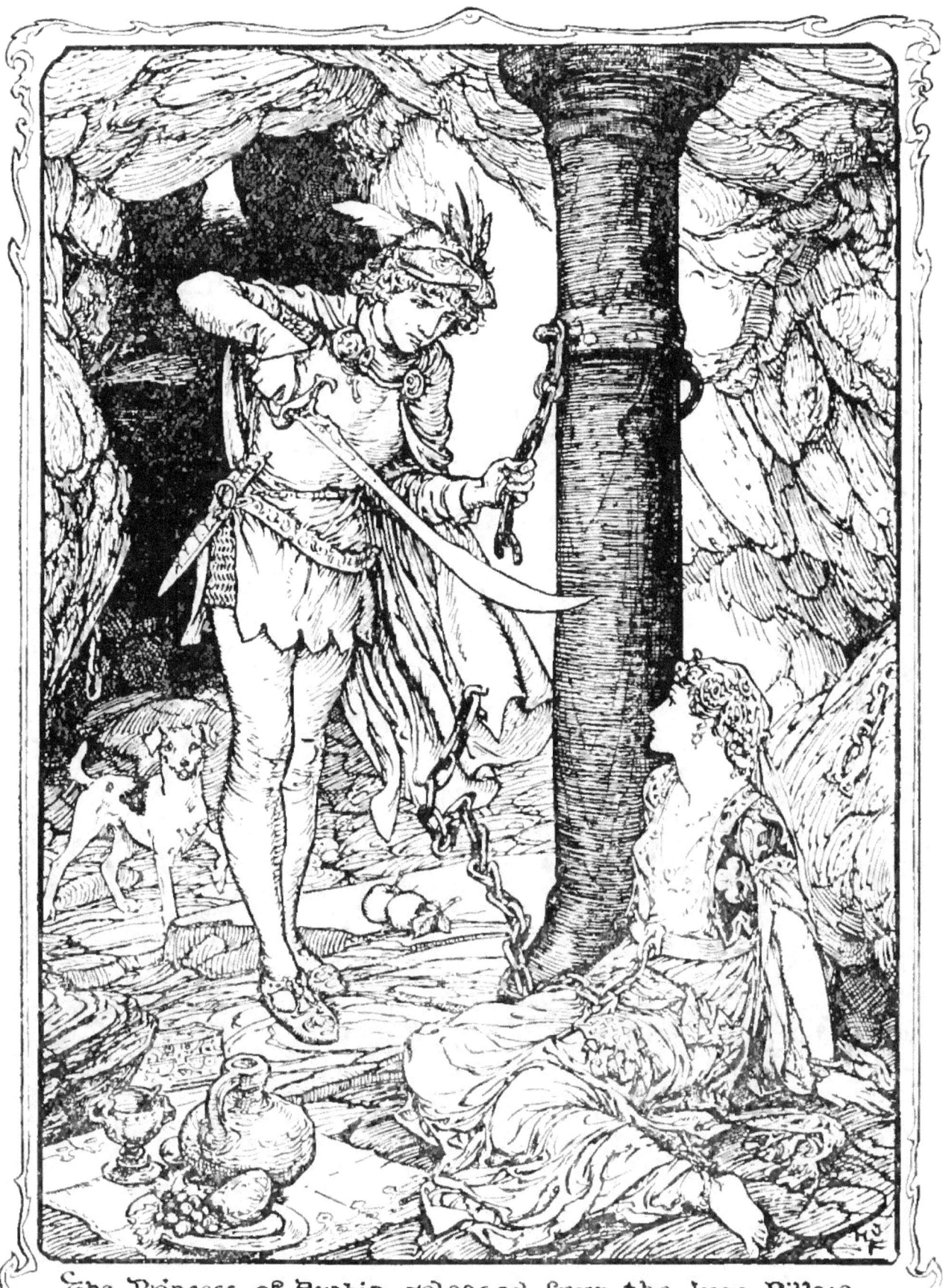
The Princess of Arabia released from the Iron Pillar

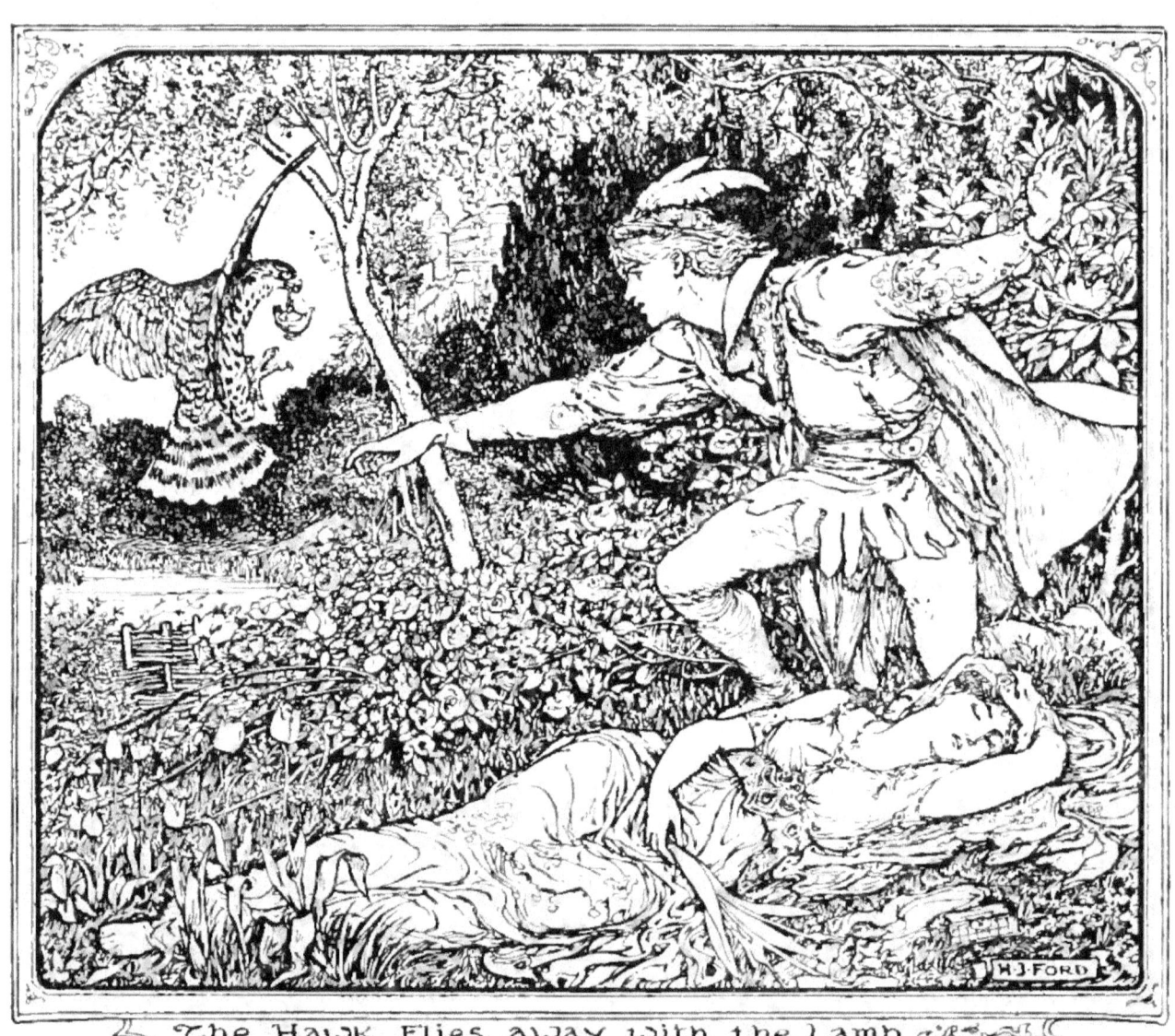

The Hawk Flies away with the Lamp

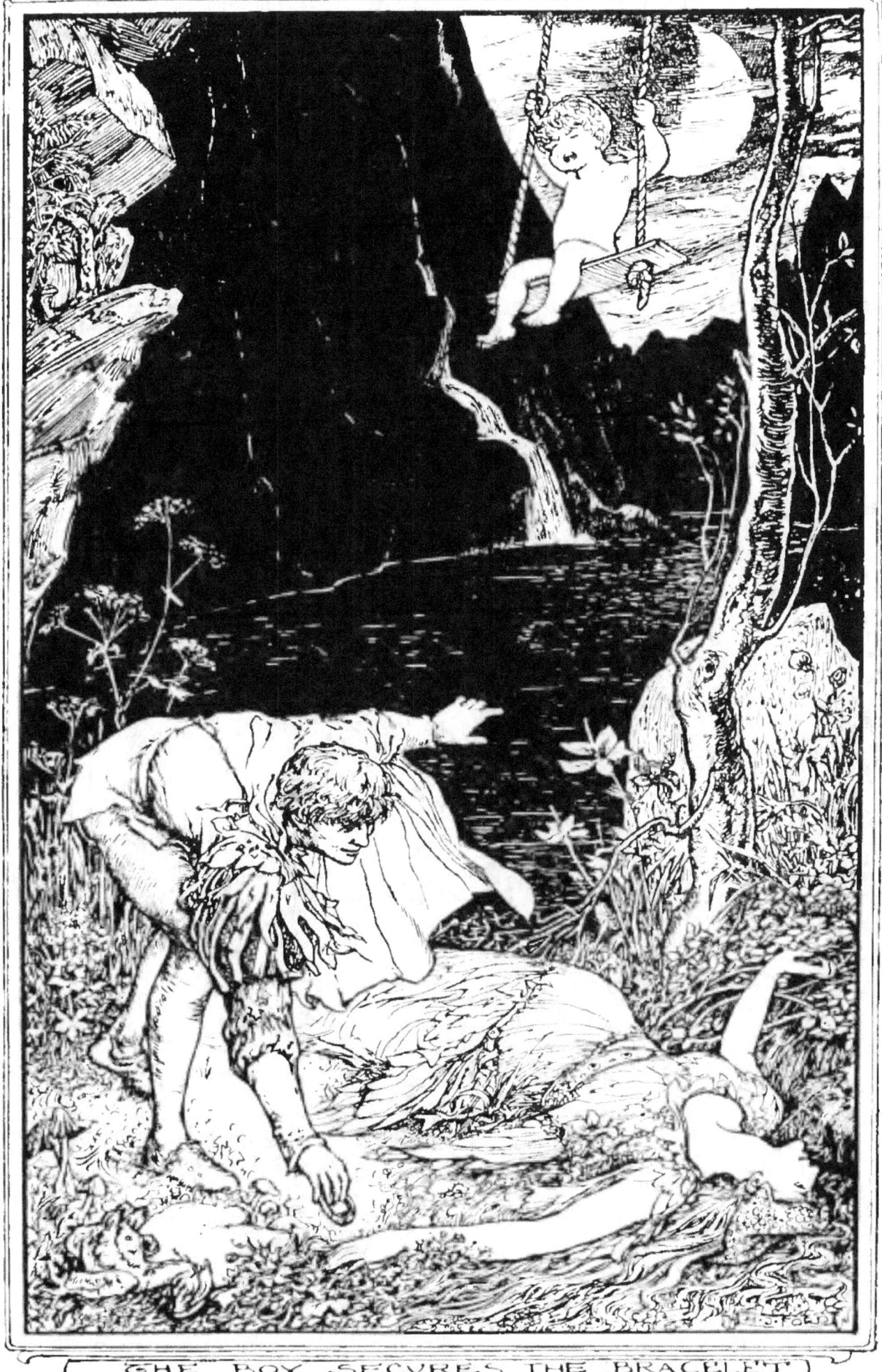
THE BOY SECURES THE BRACELET

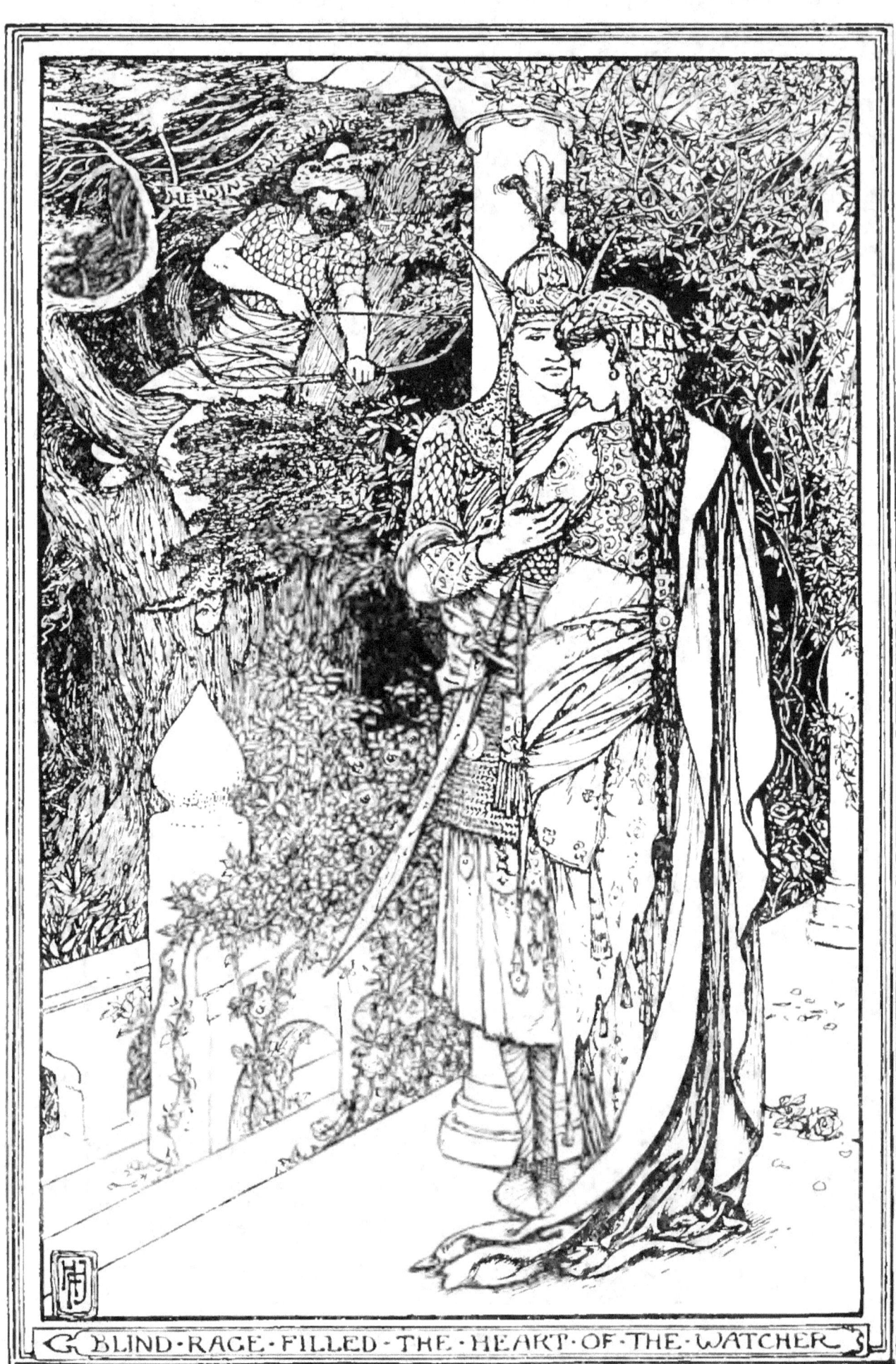
BLIND RAGE FILLED THE HEART OF THE WATCHER

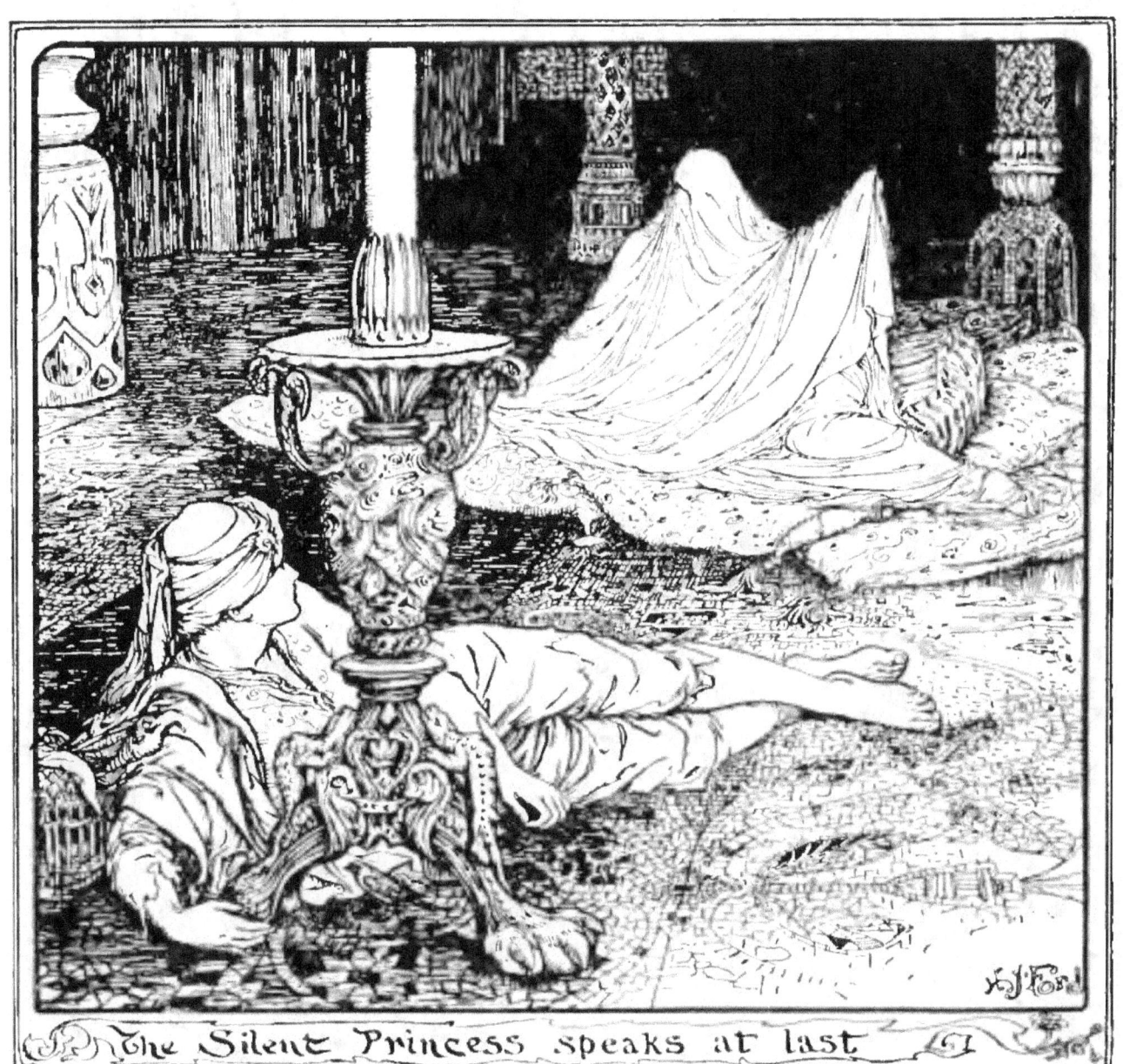

The Silent Princess speaks at last

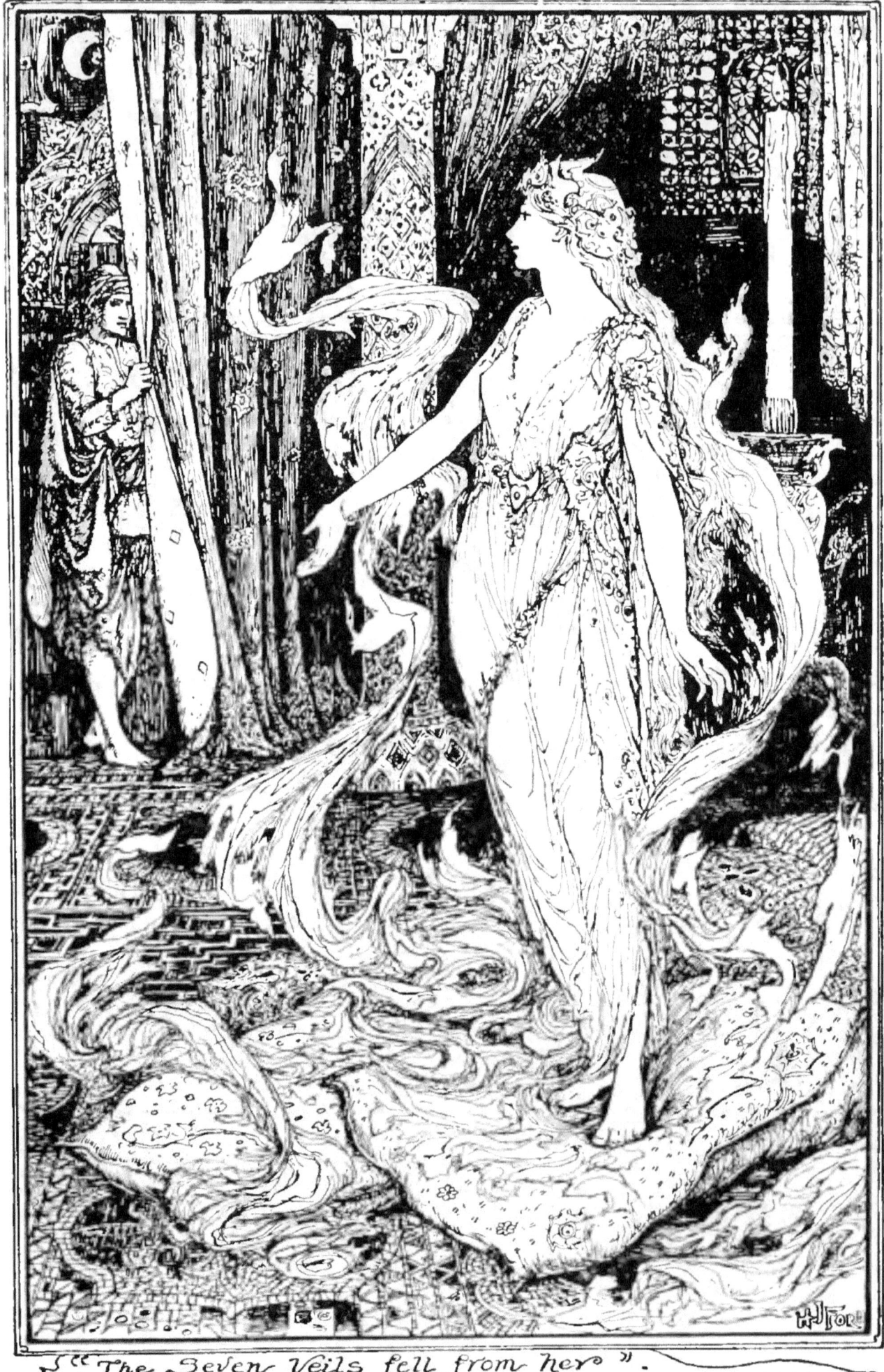

"The Seven Veils fell from her".

www.ingramcontent.com/pod-product-compliance
Lightning Source LLC
Chambersburg PA
CBHW082222220526
45470CB00010B/3274